SpringerBriefs in International Relations

SpringerBriefs present concise summaries of cutting-edge research and practical applications across a wide spectrum of fields. Featuring compact volumes of 50 to 125 pages, the series covers a range of content from professional to academic. Typical topics might include:

A timely report of state-of-the art analytical techniques

A bridge between new research results, as published in journal articles, and a contextual literature review

A snapshot of a hot or emerging topic

An in-depth case study or clinical example

A presentation of core concepts that students must understand in order to make independent contributions.

SpringerBriefs in International Relations showcase emerging theory, empirical research, and practical application in all areas of international relations from a global author community. Topics include, but are not limited to, IR-theory, international security studies, foreign policy, peace and conflict studies, international organization, global governance, international political economy, the history of international relations and related fields.

SpringerBriefs are characterized by fast, global electronic dissemination, standard publishing contracts, standardized manuscript preparation and formatting guidelines, and expedited production schedules.

Yuichi Hosoya · Hans Kundnani
Editors

The Transformation of the Liberal International Order

Evolutions and Limitations

Editors
Yuichi Hosoya
Faculty of Law
Keio University
Tokyo, Japan

Hans Kundnani
Europe Programme
Chatham House
London, UK

ISSN 2731-3352   ISSN 2731-3360 (electronic)
SpringerBriefs in International Relations
ISBN 978-981-99-4728-7   ISBN 978-981-99-4729-4 (eBook)
https://doi.org/10.1007/978-981-99-4729-4

© The International House of Japan, Inc. 2024. This book is an open access publication.

Open Access This book is licensed under the terms of the Creative Commons Attribution-NonCommercial-NoDerivatives 4.0 International License (http://creativecommons.org/licenses/by-nc-nd/4.0/), which permits any noncommercial use, sharing, distribution and reproduction in any medium or format, as long as you give appropriate credit to the original author(s) and the source, provide a link to the Creative Commons license and indicate if you modified the licensed material. You do not have permission under this license to share adapted material derived from this book or parts of it.
The images or other third party material in this book are included in the book's Creative Commons license, unless indicated otherwise in a credit line to the material. If material is not included in the book's Creative Commons license and your intended use is not permitted by statutory regulation or exceeds the permitted use, you will need to obtain permission directly from the copyright holder.
This work is subject to copyright. All commercial rights are reserved by the author(s), whether the whole or part of the material is concerned, specifically the rights of translation, reprinting, reuse of illustrations, recitation, broadcasting, reproduction on microfilms or in any other physical way, and transmission or information storage and retrieval, electronic adaptation, computer software, or by similar or dissimilar methodology now known or hereafter developed. Regarding these commercial rights a non-exclusive license has been granted to the publisher.
The use of general descriptive names, registered names, trademarks, service marks, etc. in this publication does not imply, even in the absence of a specific statement, that such names are exempt from the relevant protective laws and regulations and therefore free for general use.
The publisher, the authors, and the editors are safe to assume that the advice and information in this book are believed to be true and accurate at the date of publication. Neither the publisher nor the authors or the editors give a warranty, expressed or implied, with respect to the material contained herein or for any errors or omissions that may have been made. The publisher remains neutral with regard to jurisdictional claims in published maps and institutional affiliations.

This Springer imprint is published by the registered company Springer Nature Singapore Pte Ltd.
The registered company address is: 152 Beach Road, #21-01/04 Gateway East, Singapore 189721, Singapore

Acknowledgements

This book is the result of the second stage of the research project, "Liberal International Order," which was launched under the Asia Pacific Initiative (API) and since the merger between the API and the International House of Japan (IHJ), Tokyo, in July 2022, it has become one of the flag-ship projects of the Institute of Geoeconomics (IOG) within the IHJ. The project has been supported by the National Endowment for Democracy (NED), which was extremely generous to extend the research period after 2020, due to the spread of COVID-19 when we had just begun the second stage of the LIO project. Thus, we would like to express our deepest gratitude to the NED for its continuing support during the second stage, from 2020 to 2023.

We were fortunate to have been able to publish the results of the first stage of the LIO project in *The Crisis of Liberal Internationalism; Japan and the World Order* (Brookings Institution Press, 2020) co-edited by Yoichi Funabashi and John Ikenberry in 2020. *The Crisis of Liberal Internationalism* was widely read at the time—a time when the rise of authoritarian powers began to seriously affect the future of the liberal international order. In the second stage of the project, we decided to focus more on the role of Japan, Europe and the Quad, particularly in the Indo-Pacific region. We all feel that these actors are capable of having, together with the U.S. and its leadership role, an important influence in transforming the liberal international order.

As a co-editor, I have been particularly fortunate to have leading experts from across the globe as contributors to this volume. We have shared invaluable discussions, virtually from 2020 to 2022, on various aspects of the future of the liberal international order. All project members have been patiently waiting for the day of this publication. As co-editor, Hans Kundnani has played a leading intellectual role in the online discussions and provided an analytical framework for this book. Richard McGregor has contributed greatly to our discussion and provided an important paper that enriched our thoughts. Due partly to the merger between the API and the IHJ, we needed to adjust to many necessary administrative changes. Yoichi Funabashi is a "founding father" of both the API and this research project and, together with John Ikenberry, he provided rich intellectual insights that motivated the advancement of our second stage. Two new leaders, Chairman James Kondo of the IHJ and President Ken Jimbo of the API, have been supportive of this research project in many ways.

On behalf of the Director of Research at the API, and as a co-editor of this book, I am especially grateful to Juno Kawakami, senior editor at Springer, who was indispensable to the publication of this book, kindly providing guidance throughout the process. We have been extremely fortunate to have her advice and support. Hitoshi Suzuki, Visiting Senior Research Fellow at the IOG, who succeeded the role of project manager from Narumi Shibata, Researcher at the API, made an extra effort to synthesize all of the papers into a single volume. He has been a driving force during the last phase. Last but not least, our staff at the API and IOG who are in charge of this research project have been extremely supportive in the advancement of this research. I am grateful to all of them for their continuous and energetic support.

Yuichi Hosoya

Contents

1 **Introduction: Japan and the Reform of the Liberal International Order** 1
Yuichi Hosoya

2 **American Strategy and the Liberal International Order** 7
Zack Cooper

3 **East Asia, Europe and the High Sea: The Geostrategic Trinity of the U.S.-Led Order** 13
Luis Simón

4 **The EU's Connectivity Strategy 2.0: Global Gateway in the Indo-Pacific** 23
Maaike Okano-Heijmans

5 **Germany's Indo-Pacific Turn: Towards a Contribution to the Rules-Based Order?** 55
Alexandra Sakaki

6 **France's Indo-Pacific Approach: Salvaging the Rules-Based Order and Staying Relevant** 65
Céline Pajon

7 **India, the Quad, and the Liberal International Order** 75
Dhruva Jaishankar

8 **Countering Chinese Economic Coercion and Corrosive Capital in Southeast Asia** 83
Nithin Coca

9 **The Challenge of China for the Liberal International Order** 91
Richard McGregor

10 Northeast Asia's Energy Transition–Challenges for a Rules-Based Security and Economic Order 97
Kun-Chin Lin and Tim Reilly

11 The Liberal International Order and Economic Security 119
Kazuto Suzuki

12 The Future of the Liberal International Order 127
Hans Kundnani

About the Editors

Yuichi Hosoya is a professor of international politics at Keio University, Tokyo. His research focuses on postwar international history, British diplomatic history, Japanese foreign and security policy, and contemporary East Asian international politics.

His most recent publications include *Security Politics: Legislation for a New Security Environment* (Tokyo: JPIC, 2019); *History, Memory and Politics in Postwar Japan* (co-edited with Lynne Rienner: Boulder, 2020); "Japan's Security Policy in East Asia" in Yul Sohn and T. J. Pempel's (eds.) *Japan and Asia's Contested Order: The Interplay of Security, Economics, and Identity* (Palgrave, 2018); and *Modern Japan's Place in World History: From Meiji to Reiwa* (co-editor, Springer: Singapore, 2023).

He received the Yomiuri Yoshino Sakuzo Prize (Chuokoron Shinsha) in July 2010, the Sakurada Prize for a Book on *Political Science* (Sakurada-kai) in 2010, and the Suntory Prize for Social Sciences and Humanities (Suntory Foundation) in December 2003.

Professor Hosoya is the Director of International House of Japan and Director of Research of Asia Pacific Initiative, Tokyo. He is also a Senior Researcher at the Nakasone Peace Institute (NPI), a Senior Fellow at The Tokyo Foundation for Policy Research, and a Senior Adjunct Fellow at the Japan Institute of International Affairs (JIIA). He was a member of the Prime Minister's Advisory Panel on Reconstruction of the Legal Basis for Security (2013–2014) and the Prime Minister's Advisory Panel on National Security and Defense Capabilities (2013).

Professor Hosoya studied international politics at Rikkyo (B.A.), Birmingham (MIS), and Keio (Ph.D.). He was visiting professor and Japan Chair (2009–2010) at Sciences-Po in Paris (Institut d'Études Politiques), visiting fellow (Fulbright Fellow, 2008–2009) at Princeton University, and visiting fellow at Downing College, the University of Cambridge (July 2022–).

Hans Kundnani is an associate fellow at the Royal Institute of International Affairs (Chatham House) in London, where he was previously the director of the Europe programme. Before joining Chatham House as a senior research fellow in 2018, he was a senior Transatlantic fellow at the German Marshall Fund of the United States and research director at the European Council on Foreign Relations. In 2016, he was a Bosch Public Policy Fellow at the Transatlantic Academy in Washington, D.C. He is also an associate fellow at the Institute for German and European Studies at Birmingham University.

Hans is the author of *Utopia or Auschwitz: Germany's 1968 Generation and the Holocaust* (2009), *The Paradox of German Power* (2014), which has been translated into German, Italian, Japanese, Korean, and Spanish, and *Eurowhiteness: Culture, Empire, and Race in the European Project* (forthcoming 2023). He studied German and philosophy at Oxford University and journalism at Columbia University in New York, where he was a Fulbright Scholar. He tweets @hanskundnani.

Abbreviations

A2AD	Anti-Access and Area Denial
ADB	Asian Development Bank
AIIB	Asian Infrastructure Investment Bank
ASEAN	Association of Southeast Asian Nations
AUKUS	Australia, the United Kingdom and the United States
BASIC	Brazil, South Africa, India and China
BRI	Belt and Road Initiative
BRICS	Brazil, Russia, India, China and South Africa
CAI	Comprehensive Agreement on Investment
CNPC	China National Petroleum Corp
CPTPP	Comprehensive and Progressive Agreement for Trans-Pacific Partnership
DFFT	Data Free Flow with Trust
DSR	Digital Silk Road
ECC	Enforcement Coordination Cell
EEAS	European External Action Service
EEZ	Exclusive Economic Zone
EGC	Electricity and Gas Market Surveillance Commission
EPA	Economic Partnership Agreement
EU	European Union
FON	Freedom of Navigation
FTA	Free trade agreement
GATT	General Agreement on Tariffs and Trade
GDPR	General Data Protection Regulation
IEA	International Energy Agency
IMF	International Monetary Fund
KOGAS	Korea Gas Corporation
KR	Korean Register
KSOE	Korea Shipbuilding and Offshore Engineering
LDP	Liberal Democratic Party
LIO	Liberal International Order

LNG	Liquefied Natural Gas
MDA	Maritime Domain Awareness
METI	Ministry of Economy, Trade and Industry
NATO	North Atlantic Treaty Organization
NEA	Northeast Asia
NSR	Northern Sea Route
OECD	Organisation for Economic Cooperation
PoS	Power of Siberia
Quad	Quadrilateral Security Dialogue
RCEP	Regional Comprehensive Economic Partnership
SLOC	Sea Line of Communication
TFC	Total Final Consumption
TICAD	Tokyo International Conference on African Development
TPES	Total Primary Energy Supply
TPP	Trans-Pacific Partnership
UN	United Nations
UNCLOS	United Nations Convention for the Law of the Sea
UNFCCC	UN Framework Convention on Climate Change
WTO	World Trade Organization

Chapter 1
Introduction: Japan and the Reform of the Liberal International Order

Yuichi Hosoya

Abstract Facing the rise of authoritarian states—namely Russian and China—the liberal international order has arguably declined and retreated during the last decade. The United Nations adopted a resolution condemning Russia's invasion in Ukraine on March 2, 2022, but forty nations either voted against or abstained. Countries labelled as global swinging states or the global south criticize the liberal international order of being dominated by Western civilization. The following chapters of this book aim to find possible shared perceptions and junctures between Japan, Europe, the United States and Indo-Pacific countries, which could reform the liberal international order, giving it a more global outlook and a better reach.

The Decline of the Liberal International Order

In the last decade, the decline of the liberal international order has been continuously debated. Many point out that the liberal international order, as we know it, has retreated, particularly with the rise of authoritarian regimes such as China and Russia.

A sense of crisis was enhanced when Donald Trump was elected as the new American president in November 2017. Professor John Ikenberry of Princeton University argued that: "For the first time since the 1930s, the United States has elected a president who is actively hostile to liberal internationalism."[1] In addition to this, Ikenberry also argued that: "Britain's decision to leave the EU, and a myriad other troubles besetting Europe, appear to mark an end to the long postwar project of building a greater union."[2] Thus, we needed to ask whether we would be able to defend the existence of the resilient liberal international order even before Russia began its invasion of Ukraine in February 2022.

---

[1] John Ikenberry (2018).
[2] *Ibid*.

Y. Hosoya (✉)
Faculty of Law, Keio University, Tokyo, Japan

The decline of the liberal international order was not simply caused by the ideology and the actions of a new American president who often expressed criticism towards liberal internationalism. A much deeper problem lies in the decline of American power and influence in the international community. Thus, there are several reasons why the problem of the decline of American influence has been debated by various influential thinkers.

First, the failure of American attempts to expand democracy both in Afghanistan and in Iraq has nurtured an impression of limitations to the power projection of the U.S. The spread of the Islamic State in Iraq and in Syria, as well as the reluctance of the U.S. government to engage in the region, has illuminated uncertainty for the future of the liberal international order. With the retreat of American forces in the region, the reputation and the authority of the U.S. in the international community has been seriously damaged. It was not so difficult for China and Russia to fill the vacuum that the retreat of American forces left in the region. Russian unilateral annexation of Crimea in 2014 is one example of how the authoritarian powers began to expand their influence around them.

It is broadly perceived that the age of great power competition began with the decline of the liberal international order in the late 2010s. Given this view, it is more important than ever to observe how China and Russia expand their influence in each region in the world today.

Second, the rise of the so-called Global South has been transforming the norms and values of the international order that the West had consolidated in the last few centuries. The two most populous powers, India and China, have repeatedly criticized how Western Civilization has dominated the international order while their own values are not seriously taken into consideration. In short, it is repeatedly argued that the international order today must be more globalized now than in previous centuries when the West was able to dominate.

Even though the decline or the crisis of the liberal international order has been thoroughly debated by many commentators, it is now necessary to link it with the rise of the Global South and also the Russian invasion of Ukraine, which has seriously been undermining the liberal international order as we have known it. In this volume, we have assembled valuable arguments on the limitations of the liberal international order in a time of crisis.

Japan and Europe Defend the Liberal International Order

Having faced the abdication of global leadership by President Trump who favored "America First" policies, Ikenberry emphasizes the importance of the role of other leading liberal democracies such as Japan and Germany. He wrote in his article in *Foreign Affairs* that:

> If the liberal international order is to survive, leaders and constituencies around the world that still support it will need to step up. Much will rest on the shoulders of Prime Minister Shinzo Abe of Japan and Chancellor Angela Merkel of Germany, the only two leaders of consequence left standing who support it.[3]

Around this time, Japanese Prime Minister Shinzo Abe began to promote an important new diplomatic initiative, called "the free and open Indo-Pacific" vision. As the longest-serving prime minister in Japanese political history, Prime Minister Abe could enjoy a strong political foundation where he could present important diplomatic initiatives that previous prime ministers could not during their short terms in office.

Thus, Jeffrey Hornung of Rand Corporation wrote that, "Under the current prime minister, Shinzo Abe, Japan's role in supporting the international order has been particularly notable."[4] Hornung also argued that: "It was part of his broader Free and Open Indo-Pacific strategy, which the Trump administration later endorsed and which places more of the burden on Japan for protecting freedom, the rule of law, and market economies in the region."[5]

At the opening session of the Sixth Tokyo International Conference on African Development (TICAD VI) on August 27, 2016, Prime Minister Abe proposed to link the two oceans, the Pacific Ocean and the Indian Ocean, by promoting both the rule of law and the connectivity in and among sub-regions there.[6] He then advocated to further accelerate the economic growth of the Indo-Pacific region. While the U.S. government under President Trump began to present a more confrontational approach to China around this time, Japan defended an alternative vision both to China's Belt and Road Initiative (BRI) and to the Trumpian inward-looking MAGA (Make American Great Again) approach. As Japan's approach is both broader and more inclusive in its regional order vision, Japan's free and open Indo-Pacific vision has been embraced by leading powers in Asia and in Europe.[7]

By proposing a broader vision in the Indo-Pacific region, Japan has been regarded as a leading defender of the liberal international order. Thus, Yoichi Funabashi and John Ikenberry wrote that "it is unsurprising that the world is turning to Japan to shoulder greater responsibility in shaping the liberal international order."[8] According to Funabashi and Ikenberry, "Japan has begun taking on this mantle as the primary driver of the Comprehensive Progressive Trans-Pacific Partnership (CPTPP) negotiations after the U.S. withdrawal, and through signing an Economic Partnership Agreement with the EU." Japan has been playing a crucial role as "Japan would suffer the

---

[3] John Ikenberry (2017).

[4] Hornung (2018).

[5] *Ibid*.

[6] Ministry of Foreign Affairs of Japan (2016).

[7] Hosoya (2019).

[8] Funabashi and John Ikenberry, "Introduction: Japan and the Liberal International Order" in Funabashi and Ikenberry (eds.), *The Crisis of Liberal Internationalism*, p. 3.

greatest strategic losses" with the decline of the postwar liberal international order, as Funabashi and Ikenberry have argued.[9]

It should be noted that, with Japan's role as such, the Indo-Pacific region has become the center of global politics in recent years. At the same time, the U.S. and China are not just struggling to expand their power and interests in the region; they are also struggling to present a more attractive vision of the regional order. Japan and the U.S. have been working together to promote a free and open Indo-Pacific. Even though the emphasis and rhetoric are different, the Trump administration also published its own version of Indo-Pacific strategy on June 1, 2019—two years later than Japan began this diplomatic initiative.[10]

On 17 July 2018, Japan and the European Union signed the Economic Partnership Agreement (EPA) together with the Strategic Partnership Agreement in Tokyo. Although there existed several sensitive issues between the two sides, the EU showed its strong energy to conclude and also to ratify these agreements at the time when the American president repeatedly criticized its own allies across the Atlantic Ocean. It was generally perceived that the EU needed its closer cooperation with Japan in order to defend the rules-based international order that was under attack.

Thus, leading European countries, such as France, Germany and the Netherlands published their own versions of the Indo-Pacific strategy between 2019 and 2020. The EU itself also published its Indo-Pacific strategy entitled, "The EU strategy for cooperation in the Indo-Pacific" on 16 September 2021.[11] It became clearer that Japan and Europe were willing to take on more leading role, as proposed by Ikenberry, when Donald Trump came into the presidential office.

Between the West and the Rest

However, it should be questioned whether the liberal international order that the West had documented mainly after 1945 could be appropriately embraced by the "Rest." Thus, Hans Kundnani argues that "these documents based on liberal principles were signed only by Western powers" and: "There was no document that laid out the basis for a specifically liberal international order that was agreed on by all the world's powers."[12] Kundnani rightly argued that "it is not only in authoritarian states such as China and Russia that the liberal international order, and American 'hegemony', is perceived differently than in the West."[13]

In this way, the liberal international order must be truly globalized with a broader and stronger foundation. However, with the General Assembly of the United Nations "Adopts Resolution Demanding Russian Federation Immediately End Illegal Use of

---

[9] *Ibid*.

[10] The Department of Defense (2019), The U.S. Department of State (2019).

[11] European Commission (2021).

[12] Hans Kundnani (2017).

[13] *Ibid*.

Force in Ukraine, Withdraw All Troops" on 2 March 2022, 40 nations either abstained or were opposed to the sanction against Russia.[14] This result showed that even the most vital norms of the liberal international order are not so easily shared by all member states of the United Nations. There exists a gap between the West and the authoritarian states, thus Daniel M. Kliman and Richard Fontaine aptly labelled some states as "Global Swing States" a decade ago before Russia invaded Ukraine in 2022.[15]

Reforming the Liberal International Order

In this volume, we will examine how the current liberal international order is perceived in each country in Asia and in Europe. Unlike the U.S. and China, Japan alone does not have sufficient resources to maintain and enhance the liberal international order. At the same time, we need to face the more existential problem of how to define the liberal international order. On this issue, it is necessary to remember that the liberal international order needs to be reformed with a more global outlook. Japan is a kind of a "frontline state" and the U.S.-China structural confrontation has been defining the future of the international order. Thus, we need to ask how the liberal international order will be affected by these recent trends in global politics.

Even though the U.S. remains at the center of global politics, we should not overlook the role of other powers in Asia, Europe and beyond, in defending, and also in reforming, the existing liberal international order. I hope that this volume will contribute to addressing these discussions.

Acknowledgment The LIO Project under the Asia Pacific Initiative (API) up to June 30, 2022 and under the International House of Japan (IHJ) since July 1, 2022 was funded by the National Endowment for Democracy. I thank all supporters of this Project.

References

European Commission. (2021). *Joint Communication to the European Parliament and the Council. The EU Strategy for Cooperation in the Indo-Pacific.* https://www.eeas.europa.eu/eeas/joint-communication-indo-pacific_en

Hornung J. W. (2018). The fate of the world order rests on Tokyo's shoulder. *Foreign Policy.* https://foreignpolicy.com/2018/10/30/the-fate-of-the-world-order-rests-of-tokyos-shoulders/

Hosoya, Y. (2019). FOIP 2.0: The evolution of Japan's free and open Indo-Pacific strategy. *Asia-Pacific Review, 26*(1), 18–28.

John Ikenberry, G. (2017). The plot against American foreign policy. *Foreign Affairs* 3.

John Ikenberry, G. (2018). The end of liberal international order? *International Affairs, 94*(1), 7.

---

[14] The United Nations, GA/12407 (2022).

[15] Kliman and Fontaine (2012).

Kliman, D. M., & Fontaine R. (2012). *Global swing states: Brazil, India, Indonesia, Turkey and the future international order*. The German Marshall Fund of the United States/Center for New American Security. https://www.cnas.org/publications/reports/global-swing-states-brazil-india-indonesia-turkey-and-the-future-of-international-order

Kundnani H. (2017). *What is the liberal international order?* The German Marshall Fund of the United States. https://www.gmfus.org/news/what-liberal-international-order

Ministry of Foreign Affairs of Japan. (2016). Address by Prime Minister Shinzo Abe at the opening session. In *Sixth Tokyo international conference on African development (TICAD VI)*. https://www.mofa.go.jp/afr/af2/page4e_000496.html

The Department of Defense. (2019). Indo-Pacific strategy report: Preparedness, partnerships, and promoting a networked region. https://media.defense.gov/2019/Jul/01/2002152311/-1/-1/1/DEPARTMENT-OF-DEFENSE-INDO-PACIFIC-STRATEGY-REPORT-2019.PDF

The U.S. Department of State. (2019). *The U.S. Department of State also issued its own version of the Indo-Pacific strategy later in the same year. A free and open Indo-Pacific: Toward a shared vision*. The Department of State. https://www.state.gov/wp-content/uploads/2019/11/Free-and-Open-Indo-Pacific-4Nov2019.pdf

The United Nations, GA/12407 (2022) General assembly overwhelmingly adopts resolution demanding Russian federation immediately end illegal use of force in Ukraine, withdraw all troops. https://press.un.org/en/2022/ga12407.doc.htm

Funabashi, Y. (202). Preface. In Y. Funabashi & G. J. Ikenberry (eds.), *The crisis of liberal internationalism: Japan and the world order* (p. viii). Brookings Institution Press (p. viii).

Open Access This chapter is licensed under the terms of the Creative Commons Attribution-NonCommercial-NoDerivatives 4.0 International License (http://creativecommons.org/licenses/by-nc-nd/4.0/), which permits any noncommercial use, sharing, distribution and reproduction in any medium or format, as long as you give appropriate credit to the original author(s) and the source, provide a link to the Creative Commons license and indicate if you modified the licensed material. You do not have permission under this license to share adapted material derived from this chapter or parts of it.

The images or other third party material in this chapter are included in the chapter's Creative Commons license, unless indicated otherwise in a credit line to the material. If material is not included in the chapter's Creative Commons license and your intended use is not permitted by statutory regulation or exceeds the permitted use, you will need to obtain permission directly from the copyright holder.

Chapter 2
American Strategy and the Liberal International Order

Zack Cooper

Abstract Is the world unipolar, bipolar, or multipolar? This is a fundamental question for international relations scholars, many of whom stress the importance of structure on patterns of state behavior (see, for example, Kenneth N. Waltz, *Theory of International Politics,* Waveland Press (1979)). But on this critical issue, Americans are deeply divided. Furthermore, there are substantial differences between the views of Americans and those of key allies and partners abroad. As a result, there is a growing divide between how many Americans see the world—as either unipolar or bipolar—and how it is perceived by most others: increasingly multipolar. This has substantial implications for U.S. strategy. Most importantly, it will impede efforts to build strong and sustainable coalitions, which are necessary to bolster the liberal international order.

Differing Views of Power and Influence

Americans tend to be convinced that maintaining a military edge is important and are relatively confident in the U.S. military's current edge. In 2022, 51% of American said the United States is number one in the world militarily, while 47% said it was one of several leaders.[1] Furthermore, 68% called it important that the United States be top in the world militarily. A 2019 poll reflected similar figures, with 61% of Americans saying that U.S. policies should try to keep America the only military superpower.[2] Notably, this was a more popular view among conservatives (80% of whom supported the proposition) than liberals (only 40% of whom agreed). These

---

[1] "U.S. Position in the World," Gallup (2022) https://news.gallup.com/poll/116350/position-world.aspx.
[2] Pew Research Center (2019).

Z. Cooper (✉)
American Enterprise Institute, Princeton University, Princeton, USA
e-mail: zack.cooper@aei.org

© The International House of Japan, Inc. 2024
Y. Hosoya and H. Kundnani (eds.), *The Transformation of the Liberal International Order*, SpringerBriefs in International Relations,
https://doi.org/10.1007/978-981-99-4729-4_2

numbers suggest that a majority of the American public not only believes in the importance of American military primacy, but also believes that it still exists.

The economic situation is viewed more pessimistically by Americans.[3] Only 16% of Americans said that the United States has the world's top economy in 2022, compared to 82% who responded that the United States is one of several leading economic powers.[4] And a slim plurality of 50% of Americans say it is important for the United States to remain number one in the world economically, compared to 49% who responded that it was not that important as long as the United States remains among the leading economic powers. Yet, despite these figures, confidence in U.S. economic staying power is substantial. In 2021, more Americans said the United States would be the world's leading economic power in 20 years than thought it was the leading economic power at the time.[5] This is remarkable optimism given economic trends over the past few decades.

When foreign experts are asked to rate American military and economic power, they tend to be far more skeptical. Trans-Atlantic polling shows that European allies see China and the European Union as more influential than do their American counterparts.[6] Nonetheless, 59% of those polled in Europe still expect the United States to be a stronger power than China in ten years.[7] But the picture is worse for the United States in other regions. For example, only 29% of Southeast Asian experts see the United States as having the most political and strategic influence in their region.[8] The figure was even lower—just 9%—when asked whether the United States has the most economic influence in Southeast Asia. Surveys on U.S. influence in African countries often reflect similar dynamics.[9] In short, outside the United States there is more skepticism about America's level of power and influence abroad—in fact, many think Washington's time in the sun has already passed.

The Dangers of Misdiagnosing Polarity

Does it matter that American views of U.S. power and influence differ from those abroad? After all, one can make an argument for either a unipolar, bipolar, or multipolar world. Indeed, the United States remains by far the world's largest economy, suggesting to some that a unipolar order still exists. For example, the United States is first in accumulated wealth, with an estimated $126 trillion for 2020, compared

---

[3] See, for example, Smeltz et al. (2021).

[4] "U.S. Position in the World," Gallup.

[5] "U.S. Position in the World," Gallup.

[6] "Transatlantic Trends 2021," The German Marshall Fund of the United States and Bertelsmann Foundation (August 2021) https://www.gmfus.org/sites/default/files/2021-08/TT2021_Web_Version.pdf.

[7] Krastev and Leonard (2021).

[8] Seah et al. (2022).

[9] Ward et al. (2021).

to China with $74 trillion.[10] These two figures together account for 48% of global wealth. No other economy comes close, with Japan next at $27 trillion (6.5% of global wealth), followed by Germany, the United Kingdom, and France, each with $15–20 trillion.

These figures suggest that the United States and China are clearly the world's two largest economies (although China still stands at only 58% of U.S. wealth). Yet, this still does not mean that the world is either unipolar or bipolar. Europe, if aggregated, still has roughly $100 trillion in wealth—roughly on par with the United States and China. With many European leaders calling for greater autonomy—effectively greater distance from the United States—many in Europe argue that it must be recognized as a separate pole. The same could be true of India, which is still seeking an approach that allows it substantial flexibility, as well as a number of other major countries from Japan to Russia.

This creates an unusual situation in which many of the leading powers disagree not just on their relative power, but on the very polarity of the system itself. Such differences should come as no surprise to international relations scholars, since assessments of one's own power are often overly optimistic, even far after the point at which one's relative power has peaked and started to decline.[11] Leaders and their publics tend to focus on the metrics that show their country is powerful and influential over those that suggest weakness and decline.

For all these reasons, many Americans still view the United States as the world's leading (or only) superpower, while many abroad see the world as increasingly multipolar. But China has been catching up quickly in recent decades, implying that a bipolar world may be emerging. To the extent that Americans recognize other great powers, they are therefore likely to identify China as the main (and often only) real rival to the United States. Yet, few abroad share this diagnosis, and even some leading Americans are now starting to question whether we are in or entering an era of multipolarity.[12]

There is a growing risk that American policymakers will view competition with China through the lens of bipolarity, while their counterparts abroad perceive an increasingly multipolar world. The Trump administration talked frequently about the need to focus on "great power competition" in which the countries recognized as great powers tended to be the United States, China, and Russia.[13] The Biden administration has abandoned this terminology but embraced "strategic competition" and cited China as the "pacing challenge."[14] Both these approaches suggest that

---

[10] Shorrocks et al. (2021).

[11] Edelstein (2020).

[12] Haass and Kupchan (2021).

[13] "Summary of the 2018 National Defense Strategy of the United States of America," U.S. Department of Defense (2018) https://dod.defense.gov/Portals/1/Documents/pubs/2018-National-Defense-Strategy-Summary.pdf.

[14] "Interim National Security Strategic Guidance," The White House (March 2021) https://www.whitehouse.gov/wp-content/uploads/2021/03/NSC-1v2.pdf.

the United States sees itself and China (and less frequently Russia) as the main protagonists on the international scene.

The problem with these framings is that they downplay the role of other key countries, including a number of U.S. allies—such as Japan, Germany, the United Kingdom, France—that are crucial players in their own right. By suggesting that the world is bipolar, American leaders effectively deprive these allies of agency. Furthermore, this framing undermines what makes an American-led world most attractive to others: the notion that the United States has adopted a more inclusive approach to order-building (especially when it comes to other leading liberal states) than most previous hegemons.[15]

(Mis)Managing Multipolarity

The reality is that the current order is multipolar and growing more so by the year. Gone is the unipolar moment in which the United States had no serious challenger.[16] China's rapid economic development and military modernization have catapulted it to the level of a superpower. Moreover, a number of the world's other great powers are increasingly seeking more autonomy from the United States and China, rather than alignment with either of these powers.[17] Unlike the Cold War when most of the world's top economies were clearly aligned with either the United States or the Soviet Union, circumstances today are far different. Few countries are openly aligned with the United States or China—most are trying to maintain the ability to adjust their policies and alignments as their interests demand. This bears all the hallmarks of a multipolar system.

How must the United States alter its approach if it is to adapt to this more multipolar world? Most importantly, U.S. leaders must look to build coalitions rather than attract countries into the U.S. orbit.[18] Many U.S. allies and partners are willing to cooperate with the United States when their interests demand it, but few are willing to "choose" between the United States and China. Most countries want to maintain good relations with both Washington and Beijing.[19] The key question, therefore, is not how the United States can convince other countries to join its side in a bipolar rivalry. Instead, Washington will have to accept that different countries will align on different issues at different times.

The central challenge in the years ahead will be managing shifting coalitions composed of various poles. The United States cannot do this coalition-building on its own. After all, U.S. objectives will shift with American elections, so relying on

---

[15] John Ikenberry (2019).

[16] On definitions of unipolarity, see Monteiro (2014).

[17] Lim and Cooper (2015) https://www.tandfonline.com/doi/abs/10.1080/09636412.2015.1103130?journalCode=fsst20.

[18] Brands and Cooper (2020).

[19] Loong (2020).

Washington alone will inhibit a robust international architecture. Instead, the United States needs a small handful of countries that share its interests and values, not in one domain but in many. The United Kingdom, Australia, and Canada are all well-positioned to provide guidance as part of a central "steering group" that might advise the United States on how best to approach this coalition building effort.

But in many ways, Japan is an even more obvious strategic partner. Japan is the most capable U.S. treaty ally in the most important part of the world. Japan boasts the world's third largest economy. Japan is a technology leader. And Japan holds similar views on a range of global governance issues. For all these reasons, Japan is perfectly positioned to help the United States develop and build the coalitions needed for managing an increasingly multipolar system. Japan can help guide the United States when it needs advice, and pick up the pieces (as with the Trans-Pacific Partnership) when it missteps. But this will only be possible if U.S. leaders recognize the need to devolve more power and responsibility to other poles in the system.

The word "multipolarity" does not appear in the Biden administration's National Security Strategy, but the reality is that the world is increasingly multipolar. The faster U.S. leaders recognize and accept this reality, the sooner they will be able to develop strategies designed not to maintain a unipolar moment that has passed or win a mischaracterized bipolar competition, but adapt the liberal international order for the new reality of emerging multipolarity.

References

Brands, H., & Cooper, Z. (2020). The great game with China is 3D chess. *Foreign Policy.* https://foreignpolicy.com/2020/12/30/china-united-states-great-game-cold-war/
Edelstein, D. M. (2020). *Over the horizon: Time, uncertainty, and the rise of great powers.* Cornell University Press.
Gallup. (2022). https://news.gallup.com/poll/116350/position-world.aspx
Haass, R. N., & Kupchan, C. A. (2021). The new concert of power. *Foreign Affairs.* https://www.foreignaffairs.com/articles/world/2021-03-23/new-concert-powers
John Ikenberry, G. (2019). *After victory: Institutions, strategic restraint, and the rebuilding of order after major wars.* Princeton University Press.
Kenneth, N. (1979). *Waltz.* Waveland Press.
Krastev, I., & Leonard, M. (2021). *The crisis of American power: How Europeans see Biden's America.* European Council on Foreign Relations. https://ecfr.eu/publication/the-crisis-of-american-power-how-europeans-see-bidens-america/
Lim, D. J., & Cooper, Z. (2015). Reassessing hedging: The logic of alignment in East Asia. *Security Studies, 24*(4). https://doi.org/10.1080/09636412.2015.1103130?journalCode=fsst20
Loong, L. H. (2020). The endangered Asian century. *Foreign Affairs.* https://www.foreignaffairs.com/articles/asia/2020-06-04/lee-hsien-loong-endangered-asian-century
Monteiro, N. P. (2014). *Theory of unipolar politics.* Cambridge University Press.
Pew Research Center. (2019). In a politically polarized era, sharp divides in both partisan coalitions. https://www.pewresearch.org/politics/2019/12/17/6-views-of-foreign-policy/
Seah, S., et al. (2022). *The state of Southeast Asia: 2022.* ISEAS-Yusof Ishak Institute. https://www.iseas.edu.sg/wp-content/uploads/2022/02/The-State-of-SEA-2022_FA_Digital_FINAL.pdf

Shorrocks, A., Davies, J., & Lluberas, R. (2021). Global wealth report 2021. Credit Suisse Research Institute. https://www.credit-suisse.com/about-us/en/reports-research/global-wealth-report.html

Smeltz, D., Daalder, I., Friedhoff, K., Kafura, C., & Sullivan, E. (2021). *A foreign policy for the middle class—What Americans think*. The Chicago Council on Global Affairs. https://globalaffairs.org/sites/default/files/2021-10/ccs2021_fpmc_0.pdf.

Ward, G., Kiss, E., & Savage, P. (2021). The eagle and the dragon in Africa: Comparing data on Chinese and American influence. *War on the Rocks*. https://warontherocks.com/2021/05/the-eagle-and-the-dragon-in-africa-comparing-data-on-chinese-and-american-influence/

Open Access This chapter is licensed under the terms of the Creative Commons Attribution-NonCommercial-NoDerivatives 4.0 International License (http://creativecommons.org/licenses/by-nc-nd/4.0/), which permits any noncommercial use, sharing, distribution and reproduction in any medium or format, as long as you give appropriate credit to the original author(s) and the source, provide a link to the Creative Commons license and indicate if you modified the licensed material. You do not have permission under this license to share adapted material derived from this chapter or parts of it.

The images or other third party material in this chapter are included in the chapter's Creative Commons license, unless indicated otherwise in a credit line to the material. If material is not included in the chapter's Creative Commons license and your intended use is not permitted by statutory regulation or exceeds the permitted use, you will need to obtain permission directly from the copyright holder.

Chapter 3
East Asia, Europe and the High Sea: The Geostrategic Trinity of the U.S.-Led Order

Luis Simón

Abstract The U.S.-led international order rests on a geostrategic trinity, that is: "command of the sea," and the other global commons such as airspace, outer space and cyber-space, and the preservation of favorable balances of power in East Asia and Europe. The U.S. and its allies' powers and institutions underpin the international order, while the economic and political rise of China is leading to greater contestation of that order. The Euro-Atlantic and Indo-Pacific are increasingly interconnected, which could create a basis for Europeans to make more of a contribution to security in the Indo-Pacific. The Euro-Atlantic allies should avoid the trap of overpreparing to fight the war in continental Europe, and focus more on how they may contribute to deterring a future war in East Asia, and to the preservation of command of the commons.

This chapter zooms in on the *hardware* of the U.S.-led international order. I argue that such order rests on a geostrategic trinity: "command of the sea," and the other global commons (i.e., airspace, outer space and cyber-space), and the preservation of favorable balances of power in East Asia and Europe. These three elements are linked. Command of the commons is critical to the effective projection of military power onto Europe and East Asia, as well as to the preservation of favorable balances in those two regions. In turn, such favorable balances help keep at bay those great powers that may otherwise be in a position to challenge command of the commons.

This chapter will first discuss the link between the U.S. and its allies' power and the institutions that underpin the international order, and discuss how the rise of China and the competitive turn in international politics are leading to greater contestation of that order. I will then unpack the material foundations underpinning the U.S.-led order: command of the commons and the preservation of favorable balances in

---

L. Simón (✉)
Center for Security, Diplomacy and Strategy (CSDS), VUB's School of Governance, Brussels, Belgium

Brussels office of the Elcano Royal Institute, Madrid, Spain

© The International House of Japan, Inc. 2024
Y. Hosoya and H. Kundnani (eds.), *The Transformation of the Liberal International Order*, SpringerBriefs in International Relations,
https://doi.org/10.1007/978-981-99-4729-4_3

Europe and East Asia. This chapter will conclude with some reflections about the relative importance of Europe and Asia in the context of China's rise and the current war in Ukraine.

A U.S.-Led International Order

In his seminal work *Liberal Leviathan*, G. John Ikenberry makes a fairly intuitive point: international orders, norms, and institutions reflect power balances—they are created and maintained by powerful states or coalitions forming around them.[1] Indeed, ongoing debates around the international order's allegedly "liberal," "open" or "global" nature often gloss over its most important and defining attribute: it is, first and foremost, a U.S.-led order. As I argue below, "U.S.-led" arguably makes for a more accurate description of the current international order than simply "American," in that the order is *led* but not *owned* by the United States, or at least not fully. Other powers, particularly U.S. allies, are co-tenants, and the order's sustainability requires their active participation.

After World War II, the United States and its allies set out to develop a set of interconnected global and regional institutions aimed at "locking" their geopolitical gains.[2] Some of those institutions were rather inclusive, the United Nations (U.N.) system being arguably the best example—even though its security council was restricted to great powers, it included all the remaining ones, including America's main geopolitical competitor (the Soviet Union).[3] Others have been more exclusive, however. The so-called Bretton Woods institutions (i.e., International Monetary Fund, World Bank, and General Agreement on Trade and Tariffs, later renamed World Trade Organization), which form the backbone of the international economic order, excluded many countries for a long time (including Russia and China), and afforded the United States and its allies (mainly Western Europeans and Japan) a position of institutional and normative primacy. Even more exclusive was the so-called regional layer of the international order, with the critical regions of Europe and East Asia structured around U.S.-led alliances (NATO and the hub-and-spokes system respectively) or U.S.-sponsored institutions (like the European Community).

U.S. geopolitical and security interests were thus in sync with an international order which, by and large, excluded the Soviet Union and its satellite countries, and proved instrumental in cementing U.S. economic and political ties with key countries in the European and East Asian rimlands. The international order was therefore not neutral in power-political terms. It reflected U.S. and its allies' interests, and was

---

[1] Ikenberry (2011).

[2] For a critical perspective on the U.S.-led international order see Acharya (2018). On the importance of the regional layer of the order see Wright (2018).

[3] Admittedly, the United Nations Security Council was an exclusive great power club. However, it did include all of the great powers, including America's main geopolitical rival (the Soviet Union).

strategically leveraged by the United States in its long-term strategic competition with the Soviet Union.

The collapse of the Soviet Union cleared the path for the progressive "globalization" of the U.S.-led order from the early 1990s onwards. That was illustrated by the integration of Central and Eastern Europe, Central and South Asia, Southeast Asia, and parts of the Middle East into many of the institutions that embodied the order—and even also that of Russia and China, however fragile or selective such integration may have turned out to be. While this may have given some the impression that the order's globalization was neutral in power-political terms, it was not: it was underwritten by the U.S. and its allies' power all along.[4]

From the 2010s onwards, scholars and policy-makers have begun to debate to what extent the return of great power competition—and more precisely China's rise and America's (alleged) relative decline—may impinge on the structure of the international order.[5] Rising powers (notably China) have consistently argued that some of the order's flagship institutions—like the International Monetary Fund, World Bank, or World Trade Organization—should be reformed to reflect new political realities. In parallel, they have sponsored new institutions designed to their image, such as the Belt and Road Initiative or the Asian Infrastructure Investment Bank. This has spurred much debate as to whether the international order has become increasingly contested or rather that there are various, overlapping orders.

How did the United States and its allies manage to get such a commanding position in the post-war international order in the first place? How can they defend such position in an increasingly competitive context?

The Order's Hardware

Scholars have written extensively about the importance of sea power in international politics.[6] The sea—and more specifically the high seas—is the first and arguably most important of the so-called "global commons," i.e., those spaces that belong to no one and provide access to much of the world.[7] Command of the sea affords a great power the ability to move freely in peacetime and wartime, deny such freedom to relevant competitors, and effectively project military power on land worldwide. In Paul Kennedy's words, command of the sea allows one to exercise "influence at a global rather than a purely regional level."[8] Conversely, forward force deployments

---

[4] Posen (2003).

[5] See, e.g., Layne (2018); John Ikenberry and Nexon (2019).

[6] See, e.g., Mahan (1890); Corbett (2006); Spykman (1942).

[7] I hereby use command of the sea and command of the commons interchangeably. For a broader discussion on how they are linked see Posen, "Command of the Commons".

[8] Kennedy (1983).

and alliances have traditionally allowed sea powers to undergird favorable balances of power in key continental environments, thus holding potential challengers at bay.[9]

Over the past three centuries, those great powers who have exercised command of the sea have played a key role in structuring the international order—first the United Kingdom and later the United States.[10] Command of the sea allowed the United States to achieve the following: to project overwhelming military power into Europe and East Asia during World War II; to permanently supply forwardly deployed forces and articulate alliances in those two regions during the Cold War; to keep great power competitors away from the Western Hemisphere; and, project military power worldwide. Arguably, by ensuring a strategic edge over potential competitors, command of the sea helped set the foundations for U.S. command of the other global commons (air, space, cyber-space).[11]

Whilst command of the sea may indeed afford the United States a global strategic outlook, Europe and East Asia have traditionally held the pride of place for Washington.[12] Outside of North America, these two regions harbor the greatest concentration of wealth, industrial, technological, and military power in the world. If another great power managed to dominate either region, it would be in a position to directly challenge U.S. command of the sea. Therefore, preserving favorable balances of power in Europe and East Asia, and Washington's historical commitment to lasting alliances and forward military presence in both regions remains important.

Command of the sea and the preservation of a favorable continental balance in Europe go hand in hand. U.S. and its allies' supremacy over the main maritime approaches to the European continent—namely, the Atlantic Ocean, the Baltic and Mediterranean seas—provide the foundation for U.S. forward presence in Europe through a regional network of bases and alliances, whose main institutional manifestation is NATO. Such alliances and bases are critical to the preservation of a favorable balance in Europe. Conversely, a favorable continental balance is the best way to hold prospective challengers at bay, safeguard U.S. and allied command over the continent's maritime approaches and, ultimately, command of the sea. The logic cuts both ways.

A somewhat similar logic applies to East Asia. The U.S. and its allies' supremacy over the main maritime approaches to the East Asian rimland (i.e., through Singapore, the Philippines, Taiwan, the Ryukus and Japan's main islands) has been the foundation of forward presence in the region since World War II. Japan stands out, however, as the regional hub of the U.S. Air Force and Navy, including the Marine Corps. Australia, which provides a secure geostrategic rear, is likely to become increasingly central to U.S. force posture in the region if China's Anti-Access and Area Denial (A2AD) capabilities continue to threaten U.S. positions in north- and

---

[9] Corbett, *Some Principles*; Simms (2007). On the balance of power, see Nexon (2009).

[10] Kennedy (1983). Kennedy distinguishes command of the sea—or naval mastery—from temporary, local naval superiority, or local command of the sea.

[11] Posen, "Command of the Commons".

[12] Layne (2007).

south-east Asia. U.S.-led alliances and bases are thus also critical to the preservation of a favorable balance in East Asia. Conversely, preventing the emergence of a regional hegemon is the best way to safeguard the U.S. and its allies' superiority in the Western Pacific. This is why China's A2/AD threat within the first island chain poses such a fundamental strategic challenge, as it threatens U.S. allies and forward operating bases, upon which both a favorable regional balance and command of the commons rest.[13]

The relationship between the United States and its Euro-Atlantic and Indo-Pacific allies is symbiotic. U.S. allies in Europe and East Asia have played a particularly important role in upholding favorable balances in their respective regions. In doing so, they help free up U.S. resources and bandwidth, affording Washington greater global strategic flexibility. They also regularly support U.S. diplomatic initiatives and operations beyond their home regions, and are actively engaged in many of the institutions that underpin the international order. Moreover, their interoperability with the United States in the naval, air, space and cyber domains allows them to contribute to command of the commons. All in all, the capability and legitimacy provided by allies helps makes the U.S.-led order stronger and more sustainable.

To be sure, whilst America's Indo-Pacific and Euro-Atlantic allies may indeed contribute to the overall stability of the U.S.-led order, the bulk of their contribution revolves around their respective regions. There is indeed much debate around the fact that NATO and the hub-and-spokes alliances are first and foremost regional alliances, and have little to do with U.S. alliances or activities elsewhere.[14] An important strand of work also focuses on how Indo-Pacific and Euro-Atlantic allies even compete for U.S resources, and how the United States should prioritize between both regions and sets of alliances.[15]

Discussions about regional tradeoffs and priorities are by no means irrelevant. Yet, they often overlook the fact that there is a degree of geostrategic interdependence between the Euro-Atlantic and Indo-Pacific regions, not least considering their security architectures revolve around the same factor (U.S. power), and that U.S. strategic resources are finite.[16] Ultimately, the unraveling of the balance of power in one region would punch a hole in the U.S.-led forward defense perimeter in Eurasia, endanger command of the sea, and eventually threaten the balance in the other region, thus forcing the United States to redeploy its assets accordingly. This means that, even if the direct concern of U.S. allies in the Euro-Atlantic and Indo-Pacific is with the preservation of favorable balances in their respective regions, they also have an indirect but nonetheless important stake in the preservation of favorable balances in each other's region, and command of the commons more broadly. It also means that America's adequate management of the international order requires calibrating its engagement in both regions and in the commons.

---

[13] For a detailed discussion see Biddle and Oelrich (2016).

[14] See, e.g., Buzan and Waever (2003).

[15] See, e.g., Montgomery (2020); Kim and Simón (2021).

[16] For a detailed discussion on strategic interdependence see Simón (2022).

One thing, however, is to acknowledge that there is a degree of interdependence between geostrategic dynamics in the Euro-Atlantic and Indo-Pacific, and quite another to ascertain how interdependent these two regions actually are, or how that interdependence should affect U.S. and allied strategy. Thus, for instance, if a revisionist power were to upend the balance of power in Asia and contest U.S. command of the commons, it would still take time before the U.S. and its Euro-Atlantic allies lost command over the maritime approaches to Europe, let alone lose their favorable position in Europe. Yet, the bulk of U.S. strategic resources and attention would need to be diverted towards Asia. This could eventually leave Europe unguarded, and offer revisionist great powers in that region a window for opportunistic revision. The extent to which the United States is willing to take that risk hinges on two factors: the nature of the challenge in Asia, and the nature of the (latent) challenge in Europe. Admittedly, if we assume that the balance in both regions is structurally delicate and requires permanent U.S. engagement, then the United States should be wary of overprioritizing one region at the expense of the other. To what extent, however, does that assumption hold? In other words, how fragile actually are the regional balances in Europe and East Asia?

As already argued, the strategic importance of East Asia and Europe is justified by the fact that they are the only two regions that harbor the demographic, industrial, technological, and military potential to seriously challenge the U.S. and its allies' superiority at sea and over the other global commons. This has generally been the case since World War II, which led the United States to intervene in both regions simultaneously. Ever since, the need to prevent a simultaneous two-front attack in those key regions has been a core driver of U.S. grand strategy. Yet, the relative importance of each region has varied over time, as has their degree of geostrategic interdependence.

Most scholars and experts would agree that Europe was the center of gravity of both U.S. geostrategy and the U.S.-led international order during the Cold War. The international order was by and large subordinated to Europe because that region was the center of gravity of great power (i.e., U.S.-Soviet) competition. The Soviet Union's permanent deployment of hundreds of thousands of military forces across Central Europe represented an acute and persistent threat to the European balance, all the while Soviet communism enjoyed significant levels of societal support across Western Europe. No equivalent threat existed in Asia. China was economically weak, and focused inwards. In fact, it was the Soviet Union itself that was considered the main regional threat in East Asia. However, its relative lack of military forces in the region and long lines of internal communications meant the Soviet Union was more of a strategic nuisance rather than an actual—let alone comprehensive—threat to the East Asian regional balance.

Today's situation shows a reversal. In Asia, a rising China poses a serious and comprehensive (i.e., military, economic and political) threat to the regional balance. In Europe, NATO and the U.S. system enjoy a surplus of geostrategic depth, thanks in large part to the gains of the post-Cold War years. Russia's power is a fraction of that of the Soviet Union. Its only strength is military power, and even that has been questioned recently. Even though it may be premature to draw too many lessons from

Russia's performance in Ukraine, its seeming difficulties to hold on to its early gains in eastern Ukraine raises questions about its ability to even pose a conventional military threat to NATO, let alone a cross-cutting (i.e., political, economic, and military) threat to the European balance of power. This is even truer in light of Russia's growing economic and political isolation, and NATO's increasing geostrategic depth on the continent, as availed by eastern enlargement and, more recently, the "definlandization" of Sweden and Finland. If anything, the war in Ukraine may be reinforcing the assumption that the preservation of a favorable balance in Europe is not at risk, even if stability in Eastern Europe is. The same cannot be said of East Asia.

For one thing, China's military modernization and assertiveness has improved its regional military position vis-à-vis the United States, and challenged America's ability to freely access and move within the Western Pacific theater of operations unimpeded. Notably, the facts that China's territory hugs much of the Western Pacific, and the U.S. led defense perimeter in East Asia has little depth (unlike in Europe), puts China in a position to project its power to the high seas, and the commons more broadly. For another, many countries in East Asia are part of China's economic orbit, and value their political relationship with Beijing. Thus, whilst Russia is increasingly isolated in Europe politically and economically—and its ability to threaten NATO conventionally is increasingly questioned—China is making a serious and comprehensive (economic, political, and military) bid for regional hegemony in East Asia, and has the geostrategic standing and resources to venture into the high seas, and confidently push back against the U.S. and its allies' command of the global commons. Thus, the link between command of the commons and a favorable balance of power in East Asia has arguably become the key to the international order's fate.

The relative importance between Europe and East Asia is not the only factor that has changed and may have implications for the fate of the U.S. led international order. Another relevant change relates to the degree of interdependence between both regions, which was relatively low during the Cold War, and is comparatively higher today. This point may sound counterintuitive—indeed, the fact that the Soviet Union was perceived as the main threat in both Europe and East Asia apparently underscored the geostrategic interdependence between both regions during the Cold War. However, that point actually accounts for the low degree of geostrategic interdependence between the two regions back then. This is because if the United States felt it had to step up its contribution to one region (e.g., Europe) in response to a perceived increased Soviet threat therein, neither Washington nor its allies in the other region would need to worry too much about disattending the other region. After all, Soviet resources were also limited, and a Soviet prioritization of Europe would automatically limit Moscow's strategic bandwidth in East Asia. The sense of geostrategic tradeoffs between both regions and sets of U.S. allies was therefore less acute.

Today, the fact that the United States faces two different great power challengers in two different regions actually underscores the interdependence between both theaters, given the growing relevance of tradeoffs in the context of U.S. force posture and structure. After all, the main factor bringing both regions together is the fact that their respective balances hinge on the same factor (U.S. power). The prospect for endemic instability in Europe, Washington's pre-existing commitments in that region, and growing cooperation between China and Russia, do underscore the interdependence between both theaters. Moreover, the presence of first-rate allies still gives Europe a systemic importance that no other regions (other than East Asia) have. Yet, it is arguably a diminishing importance.

To sum up, it now can be argued that while the United States and its allies have faced a balance of power challenge in both Europe and East Asia, they may face a stability problem in the former and a balance of power problem in the latter. That puts the latter region on a higher level strategically. Tellingly, even though U.S. national security documents still refer to both China and Russia vaguely as strategic competitors, the former is increasingly seen as a region-wide and even global challenge, and the latter as a challenge to its immediate neighbor. As recently argued by U.S. Deputy Secretary of Defense Kathleen Hicks, Russia is the "acute threat" (i.e., sharp, near term and potentially more transitory); China the 'pacing challenge' ("that can bring together a comprehensive suite of power").[17] This distinction is not minor: Moscow can threaten U.S. allies in Eastern Europe but is not in a position to upset the European balance of power, let alone the global one. Yet, China can. From this viewpoint, Russia poses a stability problem in part of Europe, but poses no real challenge to the trinity, in that it cannot upset any of its core foundations (i.e., the regional balance in Europe or the global commons). China, for its part poses a threat to two of the key foundations of the trinity.

Arguably, the shift in the relative geostrategic importance of Europe and East Asia today seems to resemble the post-Tsushima dynamic in the early twentieth century. Following its defeat in the far east in 1905, Russia was de facto neutralized, thus clearing the way for Britain to redirect its resources against the one power that could comprehensively challenge the continental balance in Europe and command of the sea (Germany).

What does this mean for U.S. and allied strategy going forward?

In light of the current war in Ukraine, U.S. Secretary of Defense Lloyd Austin has recently argued that the United States "wanted to see Russia weakened to the degree that it can't do the kinds of things that it has done in invading Ukraine."[18] The relevance of such comments transcends Europe proper. By substantially weakening Russia, the existence of a threat to the European balance could be neutralized for the foreseeable future. That, in turn, could conceivably allow the United States to redirect the bulk of its strategic attention towards the pacing challenge, i.e., China's concomitant threat to the East Asian balance and command of the sea.

There has been much debate recently about how America's Indo-Pacific allies have shown solidarity with Euro-Atlantic ones in light of Russia's invasion of Ukraine. This is welcomed by Europe. However, solidarity is a two-way street. As the link between the East Asian balance and command of the commons clearly emerges as the

---

[17] U.S. Department of Defense (2022a, 2022b).
[18] Missy and Annabelle (2022).

center of gravity of the international order, Euro-Atlantic engagement in the Indo-Pacific will become comparatively more important strategically than Indo-Pacific engagement in the Euro-Atlantic. Seen through this lens, the Euro-Atlantic allies should avoid the trap of overpreparing to fighting the last war in continental Europe, and think more seriously about how they may contribute to deterring a future war in East Asia and to the preservation of command of the commons. Otherwise, they would be abandoning the first line of international politics, and devoting their energies to stabilizing a secondary region without having the ability to influence the broader systemic dynamics that encompass that very region.

References

Acharya, A. (2018). *The end of the American world order*. Polity Press.
Biddle, S., & Oelrich, I. (2016). Future warfare in the western pacific: Chinese Antiaccess/Area Denial, U.S. AirSea Battle, and command of the commons in East Asia. *International Security, 41*(1), 7–48.
Buzan, B., & Waever, O. (2003). *Regions and powers—the structure of international security*. Cambridge University Press.
Corbett, J. S. (2006). *Some principles of maritime strategy*. BiblioBazaar.
Ikenberry, G. J. (2011). *Liberal leviathan: The origins, crisis, and transformation of the American world order*. Princeton University Press.
Ikenberry, G. J., & Nexon, D. H. (2019). Hegemony studies 3.0: The dynamics of hegemonic orders. *Security Studies, 28*(3), 395–421.
Kennedy, P. (1983). *The rise and fall of British naval mastery*. Macmillan.
Kim, T., & Simón, L. (2021). A reputation versus prioritization trade-off: Unpacking allied perceptions of US extended deterrence in distant regions. *Security Studies, 30*(5), 725–760.
Layne, C. (2007). *The peace of illusions: American grand strategy from 1940 to the present, Ithaca*. Cornell University Press.
Layne, C. (2018). The Sino-American power shift and the end of the liberal, rules-based international order. *International Affairs, 94*(1), 89–111.
Mahan, A. T. (1890). *The influence of sea power upon history, 1660–1783*. Little, Brown, and Company.
Missy, R., & Annabelle, T. (2022). U.S. wants Russian military 'weakened' from Ukraine invasion, Austin says. *The Washington Post*. https://www.washingtonpost.com/world/2022/04/25/russia-weakened-lloyd-austin-ukraine-visit/. Accessed April 2023.
Montgomery, E. B. (2020). Primacy and punishment: US grand strategy, military power, and military operations to manage decline. *Security Studies, 29*(4), 769–796.
Nexon, D. H. (2009). The balance of power in the balance. *World Politics, 61*(2), 330–359.
Posen, B. (2003). Command of the commons: The military foundation of U.S. hegemony. *International Security, 28*(1), 5–46.
Simms, B. (2007). *Three victories and a defeat: The rise and fall of the first British empire, 1714–1783*. Penguin Books.
Simón, L. (2022). *Bridging U.S.-led alliances in the Euro-Atlantic and Indo-Pacific: An inter-theater perspective*. Center for Strategic and International Studies (2022).
Spykman, N. J. (1942). *America's strategy in world politics: The United States and the balance of power*. Translation Publishers (1942).
U.S. Department of Defense. (2022a). Deputy secretary of defense Dr. Kathleen H. Hicks participates in a fireside chat at the 2022a Aspen Security Forum D.C.

Edition. https://www.defense.gov/News/Transcripts/Transcript/Article/3241488/deputy-secretary-of-defense-dr-kathleen-h-hicks-participates-in-a-fireside-chat/. Accessed April 2023.

U.S. Department of Defense. (2022b). Deputy secretary of defense Dr. Kathleen Hicks' remarks on the national defense strategy and fiscal year 2023 budget request at the Reagan institute (D.C.) (As Delivered). https://www.defense.gov/News/Speeches/Speech/Article/3023001/deputy-secretary-of-defense-dr-kathleen-hicks-remarks-on-the-national-defense-s/. Accessed April 2023.

Wright, T. (2018). *All measures short of war*. Yale University Press.

Open Access This chapter is licensed under the terms of the Creative Commons Attribution-NonCommercial-NoDerivatives 4.0 International License (http://creativecommons.org/licenses/by-nc-nd/4.0/), which permits any noncommercial use, sharing, distribution and reproduction in any medium or format, as long as you give appropriate credit to the original author(s) and the source, provide a link to the Creative Commons license and indicate if you modified the licensed material. You do not have permission under this license to share adapted material derived from this chapter or parts of it.

The images or other third party material in this chapter are included in the chapter's Creative Commons license, unless indicated otherwise in a credit line to the material. If material is not included in the chapter's Creative Commons license and your intended use is not permitted by statutory regulation or exceeds the permitted use, you will need to obtain permission directly from the copyright holder.

Chapter 4
The EU's Connectivity Strategy 2.0: Global Gateway in the Indo-Pacific

Maaike Okano-Heijmans

Abstract The EU's Global Gateway—launched in 2021—goes back to the Connectivity strategy launched in 2018, and addresses the challenge of a rising China, especially its bid to increase its influence through the Belt and Road Initiative (BRI). The Global Gateway provides target states with a safer bet than the BRI and meets the infrastructure needs in the Indo-Pacific region. Based on three core principles—sustainable, comprehensive, and rules-based—the EU is able to combine economic growth with strengthened liberal values, thus maintaining and improving its global economic competitiveness and strategic advantages especially in the Indo-Pacific. The regulatory aspects of the Global Gateway are also important, as these regulations, especially in the digital domain, will have democratic values integrated within them which directly challenge the digital authoritarianism of China. Whether the EU can be successful in implementing this agenda will depend on its ability to work with the United States, Japan, and like-minded partners in the Indo-Pacific.

Introduction[1]

Policymakers in Europe are increasingly concerned with the mounting strain on the existing liberal international order (LIO) and the shifting geopolitical center of gravity to the Indo-Pacific. As the status quo of the post-Cold War era is quickly fading away, it is clear that a new, more challenging era of international politics is taking form. Leaders of the European Union (EU) and its member states are acutely aware that maintaining the previously set course will cause Europe to fall behind and hinder its competitiveness in the contemporary era. Therefore, new and increasingly

---

[1] This chapter was written in October 2021, before the formal launch of the EU's Global Gateway strategy in December 2021 and the war against Ukraine that started in February 2023. For publications by the author that consider these events in more detail, although not directly in relation to the Liberal International Order (LIO), see Okano-Heijmans (2023), Okano-Heijmans and Shah (2022) and Dekker et al. (2022).

M. Okano-Heijmans (✉)
Clingendael Institute, The Hague, Netherlands

ambitious policy programs are being devised and implemented to further European interests.

The EU Connectivity strategy—relabeled "Global Gateway" in September 2021—is potentially a central pillar in the EU's changing global posture.[2] Originally launched in September 2018, the connectivity agenda revolves around three core principles of being: sustainable, comprehensive and rules-based. This strong normative element is also apparent in the EU–Japan agreement on "sustainable connectivity and high-quality infrastructure" of 2019—which makes a thinly veiled reference to the Belt and Road Initiative (BRI) modalities as problematic.[3] Given the lagging of real progress with implementation, a second attempt to push the connectivity agenda forward came from Brussels in 2021. The agenda was then taken to the global level, and paralleled by a stronger EU commitment to the Indo-Pacific region, where the EU commits to defend and uphold the same liberal principles.

The new connectivity strategy called Global Gateway seeks to cement liberal and democratic norms and values within the international order and enhance cooperation with like-minded states. As such, it is fundamentally also an indirect response to the challenges facing the LIO. European states benefit from maintaining the current status quo. Economic liberalism, open trade policies, maintaining the principles of international law and safeguarding democracy are all crucially important to keeping Europe secure, competitive and prosperous. Therefore, the EU has a vested interest in working to relieve the strain on the LIO and help to guide it through this era of global turbulence.

Closely related to—or, arguably, part of—the connectivity agenda are the Indo-Pacific Guidelines, which are underpinned by very similar goals but targeted specifically at the Indo-Pacific region. This region is now being prioritized by European policymakers since many of the challenges to the LIO are most pressing and acutely felt in this region. The EU seeks to build on the good relations it already has in this region, pressing onwards with a more values-based approach that offers transparency and good governance to its partners, and invests in quality infrastructure, connecting goods, people and services around the world. But it is only with real political willpower and putting resources into these programs, that the EU can play an active role in preserving and reinforcing the LIO throughout this new, challenging era.

This chapter discusses the EU connectivity agenda, with a focus on the Indo-Pacific, and discusses the key challenges to achieving the EU's objectives in relation to the LIO. It is organized as follows. Section one will introduce European connectivity in the Indo-Pacific in general terms, and presents four key dilemma's that emerge in discussion of the topic in relation to the liberal international order as an overall conceptual framework. Subsequently, section two discusses recent developments in Europe—that is, the EU and its member states—regarding connectivity and the Indo-Pacific. Next, the third section reflects on partners and partnerships that the EU is turning to as it seeks to take its connectivity agenda in the Indo-Pacific

---

[2] European Commission (2019a).
[3] The European External Action Service (2019).

to a higher level. Building on these insights, the fourth section discusses the four dilemmas introduced in section one. Finally, the conclusion offers suggestions that may guide policymakers in Europe and Japan in their efforts to implement their connectivity partnership in such a way that it contributes to defending and upholding the core elements of the LIO in the Indo-Pacific, while working with partners that share its interests, and preparing for the challenges from China and the U.S.–China confrontation.

Connectivity and the Liberal International Order

The LIO has served the EU well. Since the end of the Cold War, the EU has greatly expanded by integrating the former Soviet bloc countries, enjoyed modest economic growth and international stability. However, with the return of great power conflict, economic instability, rising security challenges in Europe's neighbourhood and abroad, as well as a myriad of other issues, it is clear that the EU must step up and play a more active role in preserving the LIO. The potential erosion of the LIO is unacceptable to European policymakers, thus, the EU has constructed a policy program which will address international challenges in a wholistic manner. As argued in this section, the EU connectivity agenda is simultaneously an indirect China policy, an indirect LIO policy, a response to America's retreat from global responsibility and a core aspect of the EU's intention to become more active in the Indo-Pacific.

Although approaches and conceptualizations of the LIO seem to vary from country to country, what unifies the approaches of not only EU member states, but most liberal democracies generally, is the perception that the LIO is under considerable strain, if not in an outright crisis. In this historical movement, changing global dynamics and worrisome trends are fueling anxiety. The most direct challenge to the LIO is the rising power and influence of China. China, as a rising state capitalist, authoritarian power, is significantly challenging the rules, norms and assumptions of the LIO. Simultaneously, the United States' place in the international order is under increased scrutiny, both domestically and abroad. Faith in America's commitment to the security of its allies and its willingness to uphold the international political and economic orders is questioned and U.S. allies are grappling with the consequences of the intensifying U.S.–China conflict. Beyond geopolitics, governments around the world are under increasing pressure to address climate change, both through mitigation and adaptation. In the face of these global challenges, European law makers have attempted to construct a firm, cohesive response.

Indirect China Policy

The EU connectivity agenda and the increased attention being given to the Indo-Pacific region can be seen as an indirect China policy. It sets out to address the unwarranted consequences of the BRI and the growing role and influence of the rise of China, including within Europe; while the Indo-Pacific focus acknowledges that the challenge needs to be tackled where it originates: in China's own backyard. In the words of European Commission President Ursula Von der Leyen, the EU wants "to create links and not dependencies."[4]

The EU's current China policy, published in 2019, labeled China a "systemic rival" although it also highlighted the possibilities for deepened economic relations.[5] Since the onset of the COVID-19 pandemic in 2020, relations between the EU and its member states and China have soured. China's initial mishandling of the pandemic, the ham-fisted mask diplomacy which put Europe's reliance on China for critical goods on public display, and the inflammatory remarks made by China's "wolf-warrior diplomats" all contributed to this. The relationship saw a moment of optimism with the conclusion of the EU–China Comprehensive Agreement on Investment (CAI) in late December of 2020. However, tensions over the absence of language binding China to end the use of forced labour, especially by Uighurs in the Xinjiang region, made the deal unlikely to pass through the European Parliament for approval. The ratification came to a complete halt after China put sanctions on 10 individuals and four entities in the EU, including EU parliament members, as retribution for earlier sanctions placed on Chinese officials involved in the oppression of the Uighurs.[6]

The rise of an authoritarian competitor to the United States has put considerable pressure on democratic norms also in Europe, as China pursues its geopolitical interests with little regard for human rights and other Western values. Furthermore, China's rapid growth has rebalanced and reshaped the global economic system. The Chinese economy, which has grown at a spectacular rate over the relatively short period since it opened its economy to the world, is now at the center of the international economy. This has led to some questioning the liberal economic policies which seemed set in stone not long ago. Chinese dominance over manufacturing has given rise to discussion that European economies are overly reliant on China, which is worrying when it concerns critical goods, as the scramble for medical masks in the earliest days of the COVID-19 pandemic showed. More recently, as China has become an innovative economy,[7] Chinese technology companies are also growing in influence. These companies, in close collaboration with the Chinese government, secure growing market shares and work to export China's digital authoritarianism. This enables increased state surveillance and the ability to repress dissent, empowering authoritarian leaders globally. These trends are most noticeable in the Indo-Pacific, which is increasingly the center of international competition.

With the rise of a global power as directly opposed to Western values and interests as China, which is at the same time a crucial player in addressing global challenges such as climate change, Europeans believe that restraining rather than constraining

---

[4] European Commission (2021a).
[5] European Commission (2019b).
[6] European Parliament (2021a).
[7] John (2021).

its influence is essential to maintaining the strength of the LIO. Therefore, the EU has formulated the connectivity agenda in such a way as to address China's rise indirectly, by focusing on improving relations with partner states, engaging in capacity building and infrastructure construction and reinforcing the norms which underline the LIO. This indirect approach, which can be contrasted with the United States' direct, "extreme competition" approach,[8] plays off the EU's strengths, which are primarily economic, diplomatic and political.

Indirect Liberal International Order Strategy

The Connectivity strategy and Indo-Pacific guidelines are evidence of a shift in the foreign policy and geopolitical thinking of the EU. The EU has started to chart its own course, after years during which the growing power of China—especially as a norms and standards-setter in international politics—became more evident. Simultaneously, the great power competition between the United States and China continues to intensify. China's growing influence, and the resurgence of great power conflict has the potential to challenge the norms of the LIO. This is a threat which European states are increasingly conscious of. The EU and its member states are seeking to position themselves as a balancing power in order to protect their interests, strengthen their strategic position and reinforce the norms of the LIO.

For as long as possible, the EU seeks to avoid being forced to choose between two great powers and fall into opposing camps. Avoiding this scenario is important to many partner nations as well, especially in the Indo-Pacific. Maintaining the EU and its partners' ability to act autonomously from the two major powers is equally important. The EU is essentially attempting to put forward an alternative to China and the U.S. and give other states the opportunity to avoid being squeezed between the two. Distinctions between the EU and the other competing powers, especially China, are becoming increasingly stark, especially on issues such as human rights, digital policies and economic approaches.

As Europe is pushing for a third way, it is challenged to ensure that it remains clear that there is no equidistance from the U.S. and China. After all, the shared beliefs and strong political, economic and cultural links to the U.S. run closer and deeper. The new EU–U.S. agenda for global change of December 2020[9] acknowledges this: "As open democratic societies and market economies, the EU and the U.S. agree on the strategic challenge presented by China's growing international assertiveness, even if we do not always agree on the best way to address this."[10]

In addition to geopolitical stresses, challenges like climate change are also eroding the LIO. Many studies have shown the potentially devastating impacts that climate

---

[8] Biden: China should expect "extreme competition" (2021) U.S. AP. https://apnews.com/article/joe-biden-xi-jinping-china-8f5158c12eed14e002bb1c094f3a048a. Accessed April 2023.

[9] European Commission (2020).

[10] Ibid.

change may have in the future. Increasingly extreme weather may lead to a dramatic increase in natural disasters, food and clean water scarcity, and drive an increase in global conflict, especially in the global south. The Indo-Pacific may be a focal point which showcases the destruction climate change can bring, as many countries in the region are ill-equipped to deal with challenges like flooding and rising sea levels. This threat is reflected in the EU's connectivity agenda, which includes a focus on sustainable connectivity—including (but not limited to) environmentally sustainable connectivity.[11] The EU is working to ensure that connectivity projects live up to high environmental standards and address the need for climate change adaptation when necessary. The question of sustainability does not stop there however, as the EU also uses it in an economic manner. While Chinese projects are often described as debt-traps, due to the tenuous economic footing they leave partner countries in, European funded projects are planned so that they leave partners with manageable debt loads and useful infrastructure afterwards.

The Role of United States

The presidency of Donald Trump was a serious disruption in many ways. Unlike other recent American Presidents, Trump did not pay the same lip service to the importance of the LIO. Furthermore, the few statements he, or state department officials working under him, did make in support of the LIO were not taken seriously. Throughout the West there were doubts that Trump actively believed in the central tenets of the world order that the United States itself had been central in developing. Free trade agreements, multilateral frameworks like NATO and other core aspects of the international order were suddenly under fire from the White House. Simultaneously, Trump seemed to favor or at least accept authoritarian leaders like Russian President Vladimir Putin and the Saudi Arabian Crown Prince Mohammed bin Salman who challenged the LIO, even pointing out that the United States was not innocent of breaching international rules and norms itself.[12] This coupled with the rapid intensification of the great power rivalry with China, added strain to the LIO.

On the other hand, the Biden Administration has attempted to make a clear break from President Trump's foreign policy record and position itself as a defender of the LIO. That said, it is slowly brought home to Europeans that alignment with the U.S. under Biden will (still) have to be on its terms. This was shown by two major developments in American foreign policy. First was the U.S. retreat from Afghanistan—which was not coordinated with European allies who also have great stakes in the country. Second was the surprise-announcement of the trilateral security pact between Australia, the United Kingdom and the United States (AUKUS), which

---

[11] The European External Action Service, op. cit.
[12] Sophie (2017).

embarrassed not just France but also the EU, as it came on the exact day of the EU's Indo-Pacific strategy launch.

Secretary of State Anthony Blinken has, by many accounts, seemed to have doubled down on the international order. During the conference between American and Chinese officials in Anchorage, Alaska, Blinken opened the meeting by reiterating that the Biden Administration was committed "to leading with diplomacy to advance the interests of the United States and to strengthen the rules-based international order."[13] Blinken characterizes the preservation of the LIO as a global common good. However, the prior mention of advancing the interests of the United States may be just as critical to understanding the Biden Administration's approach to the LIO as the later signal in favor of it. The Biden Administration is being pressed to address what many see as America's faltering world power in the face of a rising China. Worries of overextension may drive the U.S. to focus more on preserving its own strength and strategic position, possibly to the detriment of the LIO. While of course the LIO still serves the American interest for the most part, Europe is coming to terms with the fact that the U.S. will not put liberal norms and values or even its most important alliances above its own interests. In addition, Europe must recognize that a close relationship with the U.S. will not necessarily bring Western countries together easily, as interests often diverge within the Western bloc itself.

America's foreign policy is critical to take into consideration as Europe has been trapped into reacting to American policy, rather than forging its own. The EU–Japan relationship is unfortunately no exception. During the Trump Administration, when America's commitment to the LIO was in serious question, there was an opening for renewed cooperation with Japan. Although this was often overstated in Europe, as anxieties over Trump's rhetoric were much more pronounced in Europe than in Japan where policymakers welcomed Trump's hard stance on China. This period was beneficial to the EU as it illustrated clearly the extent to which the EU's relationship with Japan is shaped by the United States' positioning.

Ultimately, the EU has developed the connectivity agenda as a reaction to geopolitical stress, but also as a means of becoming more autonomous from the U.S. America's recent posture has pushed the EU in this direction, in the same way as the rise of China and its growing influence in Europe has.

EU Connectivity in the Indo-Pacific and the LIO: Four Dilemmas

Adopting the concept of the liberal international order as an analytical lens, this chapter's discussion of the EU's connectivity agenda focuses on four key dilemmas that academics and policymakers face in pushing this agenda forward. These are: (1) to clarify what (element of the) liberal international order specific policies seek to defend, update or promote; (2) to reshape our own industrial policies—the domestic

---

[13] U.S. Department of State (2021).

policies that broadly inform the international connectivity agenda—without undermining the liberal and open elements of the LIO; (3) to establish interlinkages between various policy domains that have traditionally been considered separately in the LIO; and (4) to address differences between the key rhetorical devices and diverging conceptualizations governments use in relation to LIO. Each of these challenges will be analyzed in greater detail in the fourth section, after a detailed discussion of the EU connectivity strategy and its turn to the Indo-Pacific, and partners in these agendas.

Greater analytical clarity about each of these four challenges related to the promotion of the LIO is needed to bring academic discussions to a higher level and to assist policymakers as they consider potential opportunities and challenges in defending, upholding and readjusting the LIO. This certainly includes key stakeholders in the EU and its member states, as they seek to implement the EU's Connectivity and Indo-Pacific strategies with partners in the Indo-Pacific, specifically Japan and the Quadrilateral Security Dialogue (Quad).

Reflecting on these dilemmas will contribute to a better understanding of the challenges and changes which the EU connectivity agenda is attempting to address. As pressure from multiple sources mounts on the LIO and the international status quo continues to evolve in various ways, it is critical to have a wholistic perspective on the context in which the connectivity agenda was devised and is being implemented.

Europe's Connectivity Efforts in the Indo-Pacific

Connectivity policy was originally conceived in Brussels, as the primary vehicle of the EU and its member states for meeting its sustainability and geopolitical goals, namely supporting democratic ideals and maintaining the liberal international order (LIO) in the face of growing authoritarian influence. It is also increasingly being seen as a central mechanism for pursuing the EU's long-term goals: to ensure that European or Western values and norms continue to underpin the economic, political and security orders in every domain, including the crucial digital domain. As such, connectivity may be conceived as the foreign policy extension of domestic (and in the EU's case, EU-internal) industrial policies. Both are informed by the understanding that governments have to intervene more actively to protect and uphold core interests and values—that is, move beyond merely securing framework conditions favorable to industrial competitiveness, toward more mission-oriented (innovation and standardization) policies that add public value through a multi-stakeholder approach. It is thus no surprise that attempts to boost the EU's industrial policy and connectivity policy have moved in parallel in recent years, even if more concrete outcomes have been achieved on the industrial policy front.

As China policies in the West harden and become more cynical or realistic, there has been a growing recognition in Europe that the broader region, China's backyard, cannot be ignored as a region where China's role and influence is rising, while many of these countries share EU concerns and interests. It is in this geopolitical climate that first the member states and then the EU have been revaluating their position in the Indo-Pacific and the policies it has at its disposal have become more active in the region.

Towards Connectivity 2.0

In September 2018 the EU published its Europe–Asia Connectivity Strategy, calling attention to the importance of investments in sustainable transport, energy, digital and human connectivity.[14] As schematically illustrated in Fig. 4.1, the EU strategy was outspokenly normative, in seeking to contribute to "sustainable, comprehensive and rules-based connectivity" that will "contribute to the enhanced prosperity, safety and resilience of people and societies in Europe and Asia."[15] That means investments in commercially viable projects that are respectful of labor rights and environmental standards, agreed through transparent processes that guarantee a level-playing field for businesses and do not create financial dependencies on the part of recipient countries. Much like Japan's focus on "high-quality investment" and the "partnerships for quality infrastructure" that Tokyo had promoted since 2015,[16] the EU initiative may be considered a counter-proposition to BRI modalities, which—like Japan—it perceives as problematic.

Just one day after the publication of its connectivity strategy, the EU hosted the Asia–Europe Meeting (ASEM) Summit in Brussels, where "sustainable connectivity" featured high on the agenda. The EU played a crucial role in pushing this agenda, including the launch of an ASEM Sustainable Connectivity Portal—a dataset that should measure quantity and quality of connections—and a "Connectivity Inventory"—an overview of lessons learned in the field from the ASEM's activities, matched with ideas for how to improve and deepen policies and action.

A major challenge to the implementation of the EU connectivity agenda has been the fact that it came without an accompanying budget. A dedicated team of four officials, including an Ambassador for Connectivity, was installed at the European External Action Service, but this team had difficulty getting other EU institutions dedicated to key elements of the strategy, including trade, energy, digital issues and development cooperation, on board with the agenda.

An instrumental push to bring the connectivity strategy to a next level came in 2021. In January, the European Parliament (EP) adopted the resolution on connectivity and EU–Asia relations[17] following a report prepared by one of its members, Reinhard Bütikofer. The resolution called on the European Commission and the European External Action Service (EEAS) to bring the EU Connectivity Strategy to a global level; to strengthen partnerships with democracies around the world that

---

[14] The Diplomatic Service of European Union (2019).

[15] Ibid.

[16] Ministry of Foreign Affairs of Japan (2015).

[17] European Parliament (2021b).

Fig. 4.1 Focus areas and values underpinning the EU's sustainable connectivity. *Source* Okano-Heijmans and Sundar (2018)

share Europe's fundamental values; to prioritize the Western Balkans as a region and digital connectivity as a thematic focus, among other things. In response, the European Commission and EEAS in July 2021 updated the EU Connectivity strategy, referred to now as "a Globally Connected Europe."[18]

A more crucial step came in September 2021, when European Commission President Ursula von der Leyen announced "Global Gateway" in her State of the Union speech—effectively rebranding and revamping the connectivity agenda.[19] This support from the highest-level of EU politicians means that the EU institutions are now more incentivized to act.

The revamp is to be formalized with the forthcoming Joint Communication on Global Gateway (November 2021), whereby the EU seeks to improve its ability to pursue its economic, foreign, and development policy goals while safeguarding its security interests and promoting European ideals abroad. Still, substantial funds need

---

[18] European Council of European Union (2021a).

[19] Lau and Cokelaere (2021), European Commission (2021b).

to be allocated to infrastructure projects, digital development cooperation projects (to build capacity in partner countries), and regulatory dialogues.

The new Global Gateway initiative sets out to increase the number of large-scale, and highly visible physical infrastructure projects which European actors can participate in, while ensuring that sustainable financing and environmental impacts do not fall to the wayside. These projects will be built in cooperation with multilateral institutions like the International Monetary Fund and the European Investment Bank, partners in the private sector and with public financing tools. However, in addition to physical infrastructure the new connectivity strategy also calls for efforts to improve and invest in regulatory frameworks which will maintain a level playing field, incentivize investment and safeguard the international norms. These regulatory frameworks are intended to back up democratic values and the continuation of the rules-based economic order.

While the EU connectivity agenda in its early years focused much on (land) transport, the digital and energy agendas became more prominent recently—paralleling the EU's efforts towards an industrial policy that "would support the twin transitions to a green and digital economy, make EU industry more competitive globally, and enhance Europe's open strategic autonomy."[20]

Digital connectivity is the more normative of the two domains, as it ties into the deepening technology and data conflict, setting standards that will govern the digital societies of the future. Unsurprisingly, the EU's directorate-general for communications networks, content and technology (DG Connect) has come to play a bigger role in the connectivity agenda. And high-ranking EU officials throw their weight behind this. For example, European Council President Charles Michel participated in the Tallinn Digital Summit of September 2021 that pushed trusted connectivity as the European value proposition.[21] The concept of trusted connectivity is to highlight "the nexus between cross-border infrastructure, geopolitics, and digital technologies," with transparency and accountability as two "non-negotiable pillars." A clear distinction was made between like-minded partners with democratic systems—whose democratic communication architecture is diverse and enables freedom—and autocratic regimes. This proposition and concept clearly draws on Japan's push for data free flows with trust (DFFT) across borders that was set out in the G20 Osaka Leaders Declaration under the G20 Japanese Presidency in 2019.

Restraining but Not Containing China

The EU wants to address the rising influence and power of China globally, and policymakers see the connectivity agenda as a means to do so indirectly. The intention is for the Connectivity strategy to deliver tangible benefits for partner states in the region, which includes sustainable financing for much needed infrastructure

---

[20] European Commission (2022).
[21] European Council of European Union (2021b).

projects and aid in strengthening relations and democratic ideals in the Indo-Pacific. A key consideration of the connectivity agenda is the need to respond to the Belt and Road Initiative (BRI) which China launched in 2013. While assisting in the development of third countries, the BRI is primarily promoting China's foreign policy goals and bilateral partnerships, tying those countries closer to China by furthering interoperability and compatibility of their economic and regulatory systems as well as political links—if not dependencies. The contrast between the BRI and the connectivity agenda should be clear here. While Chinese investments more often come with unsustainable debt loads and possible authoritarian influence, the EU hopes to offer an alternative to states in the region, which delivers similar benefits without the risks attached. Simultaneously, the connectivity agenda seeks to improve the EU's position in the Indo-Pacific and safeguard liberal values.

The BRI and the connectivity agenda compete in various areas, including non-traditional infrastructure. The Health Silk Road is intended to boost the healthcare infrastructures and plays on China's strength in manufacturing healthcare products.[22] More concerning is the Digital Silk Road (DSR) which focuses on digital connectivity.[23] The DSR has many focuses ranging from investing in and constructing telecommunications networks or enabling Chinese e-commerce and mobile payment systems to proliferate in other countries. Although the success of the projects has been hotly debated and the impact of the COVID-19 pandemic has not yet come into focus, the BRI has nonetheless caused anxiety among western policymakers.

For several years, the EU stood by as the BRI facilitated partnerships—and with that, the growing and influential relationship of the Chinese government with other countries. Many states in the Indo-Pacific and within the EU itself—mostly in Central and Eastern Europe, but also Italy—have signed memorandums of understanding (MoUs) with China agreeing to cooperate on the BRI. The chagrin of many in Brussels about individual EU member states signing BRI MoUs lies in the MoUs' potential to align these countries' priorities with those of China.[24] This potentially undermines EU unity and cooperation, for instance when the EU negotiates with China directly or when it wants to speak out about Chinese actions in the South China Sea or in Hong Kong. More recently, the challenge to EU internal unity diminished as Chinese promises often remained unfulfilled. Poland, for example, is highly disappointed with the slow and ineffective progress of bilateral cooperation.

In recent years, the Digital Silk Road has perhaps become the element of the BRI that is the most direct challenge to the EU's global goals. And with these digital economy products, advanced surveillance technology and smart city technology is also being sold, giving authoritarian-leaning leaders new tools for cracking down on dissent. Rather than authoritarian norms and standards, the EU wants to actively push for democratic ideals to be integrated into digital technology, all of which shows the need for a comprehensive response to the BRI. China's current foreign policy

---

[22] Escober (2020).
[23] Kurlantzick and West (2020).
[24] Maaike and Tomoki (2019).

engagement is directly challenging norms of the LIO, going directly against the interest of the EU, Japan and other democratic nations.

The success of the BRI and the rise of China's influence and power generally has caused the EU and other western actors to reconsider development and infrastructure investment. In response to the BRI and the recognition for the need to invest large sums into global economic stimulus following the COVID-19 pandemic, a number of new international investment programs have been established. The Blue Dot Network was the first project but it has largely been replaced by the Build Back Better World program which was launched by the G7 in June of 2021.[25] The newly updated EU connectivity agenda seeks to contribute to this.

In order to secure democratic norms and the rules-based international system, it is essential that democratic states are also active in traditional and non-traditional infrastructure projects, especially in the Indo-Pacific. Assisting in this capability building has a myriad of benefits both for Europe and the states in the Indo-Pacific. Following through on the connectivity agenda will give states a third option other than working with either China or the United States, helping them to avoid the pressures of getting caught in the middle of geopolitical struggles. Having dropped out of the Trans-Pacific Partnership, the U.S. has, in effect, opened space for the EU as a partner for Indo-Pacific countries.

More European activity in the Indo-Pacific can also be positioned as a bulwark to block further authoritarian influence. This is especially pronounced in the field of digital connectivity and digital development cooperation. As China continues to spread its digital authoritarianism, in direct opposition to the norms of the LIO, the EU is investing increasingly more in partnerships with like-minded partners—especially in the Indo-Pacific—and becoming more active in putting forth democratic alternatives.

Connectivity Partnerships

The EU considers strategic connectivity partnerships, as well as multi-country projects with key partners, essential to achieve its goal of sustainable and secure connections. Hence, from the outset the EU has strived to build partnerships with key countries in the region, specifically Japan and India, as well as the Association of Southeast Asian Nations (ASEAN).

In September 2019 the EU and Japan concluded a Partnership on Sustainable Connectivity and Quality Infrastructure—the EU's first partnership of this kind with a non-EU country.[26] The partnership followed logically from the value propositions that both sides had presented earlier, in contrast to China's BRI. This document notably contained various normative elements, tied to the shared values which are embedded in the EU and Japan's approach and acceptance of the LIO. Next to its

---

[25] Steve and Michael (2021).
[26] The European External Action Service (2019).

strong normative element, the agreement was notable for its mention of the Indo-Pacific—the first time for the EU to do so in an official document. Two years on, the challenge of moving from rhetoric to practice is evident: the EU–Japan partnership has failed to deliver substantial results; a (forthcoming) study that is to identify possible joint/coordinated projects in Central Asia is perhaps its most tangible output.

After Japan, a Connectivity Partnership was forged with India at the May 2021 EU–India summit.[27] In addition, agreements with the ASEAN—building on the EU–ASEAN joint ministerial statement on connectivity of December 2020—and the Mekong River Delta, as well as partnerships with the United States are being discussed, while South Korea is said to be also of potential interest.

The connectivity partnerships serve as a framework for further practical cooperation by the EU and its partners, focusing on issues like infrastructure, energy, the digital domain and transportation. The partnerships also look to adopt, promote and advance mutually shared rules governing core matters like trade, investment and sustainability, and to leverage existing bilateral and multilateral channels like the G7, G20, Organisation for Economic Cooperation (OECD), European Bank of Reconstruction and Development (EBRD) and Asian Development Bank (ADB) to advance this fundamental objective.

Summing up, it can be asserted that the connectivity agenda primarily aims to defend, promote and update the economic liberal order, as well as the political liberal order. The EU is effectively seeking to use its economic leverage to become a more active reinforcing agent for the LIO. This approach plays on the EU's strength and seeks to transform it into a more effective political power with the capacity to safeguard the LIO.

The EU's Turn to the Indo-Pacific

In 2020 the EU set out to devise its own Indo-Pacific strategy, following policy papers put out by France, Germany and the Netherlands, respectively. Different from the connectivity agenda, this refocusing on the Indo-Pacific has been largely driven by a bottom-up, member states-led push to engage more comprehensively and cohesively with the crucially important region. Each policy document called on the EU to improve its posture towards the Indo-Pacific and focuses on crucial policy areas such as security, ensuring deepening economic relations with the rapidly emerging economies and effectively pursuing common goods like tackling climate change and poverty reduction. Turning points for European engagement with the Indo-Pacific came in 2019 and 2020, when the concept was mentioned for the first time in an official EU document: the EU–Japan Connectivity Partnership. The need to act on the Indo-Pacific became evident as the United States engaged more with the concept, and the adoption by ASEAN of the ASEAN Outlook on the Indo-Pacific showed the possibility of doing so without a politicized or confrontational approach.

---

[27] European Council of European Union (2021b).

What is significant today is that the EU and its member states are willing to accept the Indo-Pacific as a political construct. They were hesitant to do so earlier, when only France—with its particular set of assets, interests and capabilities in the region—started to engage with the concept, and when the Japan-initiated Free and Open Indo-Pacific vision became more confrontational towards China as the U.S. under President Donald Trump got on board with the concept.

The EU connectivity agenda is one of seven priority areas in the EU's strategy in the Indo-Pacific of September 2021.[28] This may be a logical outcome from negotiations informed by the Indo-Pacific policy documents released by member states, each of which has given attention to furthering the connectivity agenda. Many activities, like improving infrastructure or trade relationships are mutually beneficial to the goals outlined in the connectivity agenda and the council conclusions on the EU Indo-Pacific strategy.

International trade is obviously crucially important for the connectivity agenda and individual European countries, many of which pride themselves on being strong trading nations. However, China's disregard for international law, especially in the South China sea, could very well be a threat to Europe's continued growth and stability in the coming years. Therefore, it is increasingly clear, from the Indo-Pacific strategies and the actions of several EU member states, that European countries are increasingly willing to be actively involved in maritime security beyond European waters. This willingness extends to a range of security issues, from freedom of navigation to the preservation of crucially important undersea cables.

A significant manifestation of this willingness is the increasing willingness of European governments to engage in "naval signaling" in conjunction with other allies in the region. In 2021, the region will have seen "two frigates, one helicopter carrier and a nuclear-powered submarine" deployed by the French, German and Dutch navies, "in addition to the 12 ships based in French overseas territories."[29] The deployment of these European frigates is a clear sign that Western countries and their partners in the Indo-Pacific are now ready to act to uphold freedom of navigation in international waters and protect "open societies," in support of regional partners that share European values. Clearly, challenges to free navigation in the critically important shipping lanes running through the contested waters harm trade and transport connectivity.

Such moves remain controversial among significant parts of the European establishment for being potentially provocative and unnecessarily antagonistic towards China. This explains why the Germans sought to have their frigate make port in Shanghai—a move that China eventually blocked.[30] European military naval presence in the Indo-Pacific region may continue to be rare, and efforts "to guarantee safe passage and maritime security" will likely focus on other types of action. However, the EU Indo-Pacific Strategy explicitly states that the EU and its member states

---

[28] European Commission (2021c).

[29] Marc et al. (2021).

[30] China denies port visit by German warship. (2021) *Deutsche Welle.* https://www.dw.com/en/china-denies-port-visit-by-german-warship/a-59190643. Accessed April 2023.

will attempt to make more joint exercises and port calls in the future and engage in capacity building for experts in the area of the international law of the sea. Specifically, the EU has outlined building maritime capacity against drug trafficking, human trafficking, wildlife crime and illicit financial flows as priority areas.

Enhancing Digital Connectivity in the Indo-Pacific

Within the Indo-Pacific, there is another field where the EU and its member states may be most willing and able to effectively act. This is the critically important and increasingly contested high-tech and digital domain. Here, European actors can contribute to an open, safe and inclusive digital connectivity and engage with the thriving digital economies in the Indo-Pacific. For one, the Netherlands—as per its Indo-Pacific Guidelines—intends to encourage further cooperation on digital technologies, enable the increased integration of digital economies and address the rising threat of cyber-attacks.[31]

Acting in this increasingly contested domain is not only in the EU's political and economic interest, but it will work to counter China's authoritarian influence in these domains. For this reason, the focus in this discussion of EU engagement with the Indo-Pacific will be on EU efforts in digital connectivity, while transport, energy and human connectivity will be less discussed.

The Indo-Pacific is home to the fastest growing digital economies in the world. Therefore, the potential economic benefits of improving digital connectivity between the EU and the Indo-Pacific are immense. At home, the EU can already begin to make this a reality by actively pursuing policies which support European start-ups and supporting projects like Gaia-X, which seeks to develop common requirements for an open, transparent and secure European data infrastructure and encourage the growth of European champions. In third countries, the EU seeks to be active in further developing and promoting a third way, between the American and Chinese digital models. While the American model prioritizes economic growth above all and the Chinese model supports increased state control and surveillance, Europe has adopted a human-centered model which prioritizes privacy and fairness. The "Brussels effect" has already been applied successfully to push for democratic standards in digital technology, specifically in data protection and privacy. The General Data Protection Regulation (GDPR) has effectively become a global standard as many countries around the world have based their own data regulations on it. Europe can build on this success and exert further democratic influence in this domain.

The digital domain is crucial because it gives the EU avenues to reinforce the political and economic liberal order simultaneously. Promoting a human-centered approach, enforced through good regulatory practice, will safeguard the political liberal order from authoritarian influence. Meanwhile, improving digital connectivity

---

[31] Government of Netherlands (2020).

with the Indo-Pacific has the potential to produce significant economic growth for both regions, while remaining within the bounds of the liberal economic order.

EU Connectivity Partners in the Indo-Pacific

The EU connectivity agenda is especially important in the Indo-Pacific. As previously mentioned, this connectivity is one of seven priority areas within the EU Indo-Pacific Strategy. Therefore, it is important to take the region into consideration when looking at the connectivity agenda wholistically. An increasingly active posture of the EU and its member states is being welcomed by many states and policymakers in the Indo-Pacific region. A key question, however, is which countries and multilateral fora are the EU's main partners to cooperate, coordinate and synergize with to ensure that the Indo-Pacific region remains free and open, despite the global political turbulence, in the coming years and, what do these partners expect of the EU?

The EU and its partners are beginning from a similar place, characterized by mutual commitment to the U.S.-based alliance system, desire for open trade, and anxiety concerning the current health and viability of the LIO. However, these similarities do not erase the differences in approaches.

Indian experts have been particularly outspoken, expressing the wish that European engagement in the Indo-Pacific be strategically autonomous and informed by a genuine will to engage in the region, rather than about alignment and management of relations with the U.S. Meanwhile, ASEAN elites watch with caution the EU's engagement with the "Quad" dialogue, as any formal linkage with the grouping will be considered too contentious.

A critical challenge the EU faces in implementing its connectivity agenda and Indo-Pacific strategy with partners that share an interest in upholding the LIO, is to align policies despite differences in approaches and prioritization of various domains and regions. Figure 4.2 illustrates this schematically with reference to changing views on China.

Until just a few years ago, France, Germany and the EU generally took a very collaborative approach towards China, with few limits to engagement. The economic opportunities outweighed possible national security threats, which were scarcely considered at the time. This dismissal of potential downsides was amplified by the geographical distance and strong internal focus of the EU. Compared to European countries, countries in the Indo-Pacific (most notably Japan, India and Australia) started from a less open position. These states maintained a position of conditional engagement and have assessed China's behavior as assertive or even aggressive for much longer than Europe. Today, there seems to be a strong consensus on conditional engagement with China, both within and beyond the Indo-Pacific, wherein cooperation is not ruled out, but care is taken not to align one's own priorities with those of the Chinese government or the Communist Party. The EU and its member states now also consider China's behavior as (somewhat) aggressive and are wary of indirectly aiding China in growing its global stature.

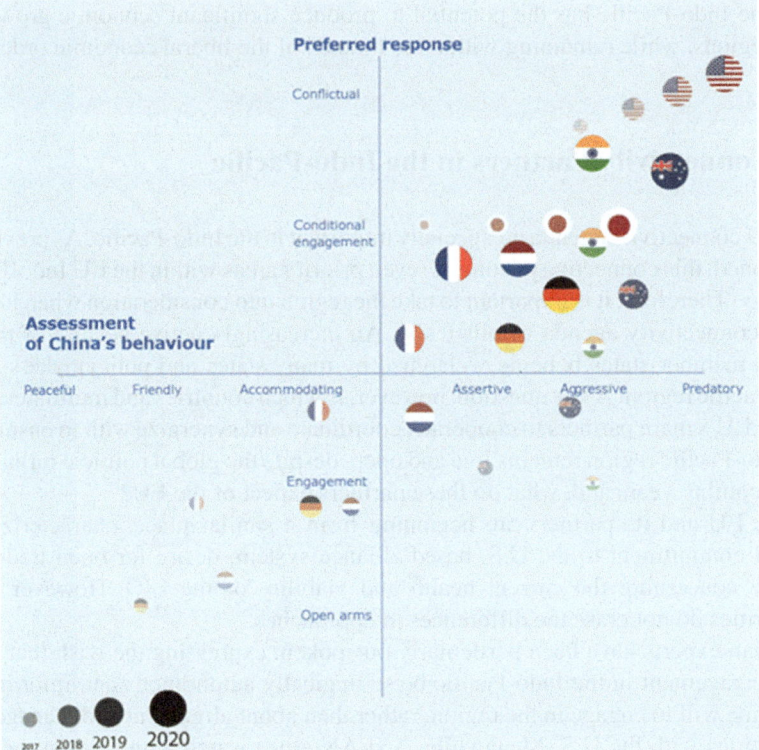

Fig. 4.2 Assessment of China's behaviour and the preferred response of various governments. *Source* Dekker and Okano-Heijmans (2020)

However, as both the starting points and intensity of change differ, current stances obviously still vary. The U.S. stands in lonely distance from the other countries, (publicly) assessing China's behavior as predatory and taking an outright conflictual approach. Clearly, these differences complicate cooperation, coordination and synergies between partners.

Go-To Partners in the Region

Japan is one of the EU's most important strategic partners in the Indo-Pacific region. The two actors have a shared interest in reinforcing the LIO and ensuring that the pillars of the LIO are upheld in the Indo-Pacific and globally. Both the EU and Japan are also key allies in the American-centred alliance system, and as such the United States plays a significant role in shaping the EU–Japanese relationship, as previously mentioned.

Beyond Japan, the most important partners that the EU and EU member states seek to cooperate with are India and ASEAN—the two that the EU has established connectivity partnerships with and receive most mention in the EU Indo-Pacific strategies. ASEAN is mentioned 31 times and India is mentioned 32 times and Japan is mentioned 22 times in the EU Indo-Pacific Strategy (compared to China, which is mentioned eighteen times). Other notable countries include South Korea (mentioned 14 times), Australia (mentioned 12 times), and New Zealand (mentioned eight times), which are also explicitly mentioned as like-minded partners, as are Indonesia (mentioned 13 times), Singapore (mentioned eight times), Taiwan (mentioned five times) Malaysia (mentioned six times), and Vietnam (mentioned seven times). The EU Indo-Pacific Strategy states that the bloc will prioritize engagement with countries that have Indo-Pacific strategies. Not only did this serve as a discrete means of prioritizing certain partners, like Japan and Australia, but it also served as a means of excluding China.

Cooperating with the United States

Since President Obama's "pivot to Asia" the United States has been attempting to reprioritize the Indo-Pacific as a focal point of its foreign policy. This will increasingly impact Europe's approach to the region as well. Many states, Japan included, currently, and will continue, to prefer cooperation with the United States as they remain by far the most important ally, especially when the rising power of China is concerned. As America withdraws from Afghanistan, and the Middle East generally, it is likely that the Indo-Pacific will increase in prominence in America's foreign policy.

Already, numerous Biden Administration members have made trips to the Indo-Pacific, including Vice-President Kamala Harris who visited in August 2021. In a major policy speech in Singapore,[32] Harris laid out America's approach to the Indo-Pacific, which is much more directly focused on countering China than the Indo-Pacific strategies put out by the EU or its member states. Vice-President Harris emphasized the importance of upholding the UN Convention on the Law of the Sea (UNCLOS) and directly called out China for its misdeeds in the South China sea, while highlighting the fact that the United States is attempting to become more involved in security concerns in this theatre. Previously the EU–Japan relationship benefited from both being closely aligned on UNCLOS, more so than the U.S. and Japan. However, as America adjusts its position, it may have taken the EU's momentum on this file. The United States is also deepening relations with key states. To illustrate, Harris visited Vietnam after Singapore.[33] In the decades since America's intervention in Vietnam, relations have dramatically improved, and the two former rivals have signed a strategic partnership. Assistance in global health matters in

---

[32] White House (2021a).
[33] Associated Press (2021).

the Indo-Pacific is also being highlighted, by the announcement of a new Centers for Disease Control and Prevention Southeast Asia regional office. In addition, the United States will engage increasingly in "vaccine diplomacy" by helping Southeast Asian countries with their vaccine rollouts.

Notably, the United States seems willing to step into security matters in the Indo-Pacific and take on new security commitments, even if it means stepping on European toes. In September 2021, Washington announced a new "AUKUS" technology-sharing working group with the U.K. and Australia, primarily aimed at sharing nuclear submarine technology. The deal came after Australia grew tired of delays and other troubles with a previous deal for submarine technology made with France. In response, France strongly criticized both Australia and the United States harshly, cancelled diplomatic events and recalled their ambassadors from Washington and Canberra. French Foreign Minister Jean-Yves Le Drian went so far as to say, "This unilateral, brutal, unpredictable decision is a lot like what Mr. Trump did."

Although tensions between the United States and France seemed to simmer down after a phone call between Presidents Macron and Biden and the two sides agreed to launch EU–US consultations on the Indo-Pacific[34] in October 2021, with the aim to step up transatlantic cooperation and joint engagement in the region, questions remain for the future of European–American cooperation in the region. Firstly, tensions between France and Australia and the U.K. seem to be more difficult to overcome, despite Australia being especially important for Europe in the Indo-Pacific. Secondly, it is notable that this dispute began between the United States and the European state most focused on security issues (versus Germany's more economical approach). It may be the case that the United States would prefer that European states focus more on security cooperation in Europe and on issues within the European neighborhood while leaving security matters in the Indo-Pacific to the United States. Also considering limitations to EU military capabilities and contestation over those being taken to the Indo-Pacific, a focus of EU action on connectivity—with a focus on the contested digital domain—in the Indo-Pacific, seems in place.

Engaging with Networks: Quad, NATO

While foreign countries, especially in Asia, took a significant interest in the turn of EU member states and the EU to the Indo-Pacific, the Dutch Indo-Pacific Guidelines did not spark much debate in the Netherlands and the launch of the EU strategy on the Indo-Pacific in September was clearly overshadowed by the surprise announcement of the trilateral security pact between Australia, the United Kingdom and the United States (AUKUS). Policymakers in Europe are still confronted with a situation wherein Quad meetings garner greater attention than their own actions. This was evident from the fact that while the Indo-Pacific Guidelines received no attention in the Dutch Parliament, the first Summit Meeting of the Quad on 12 March 2021 sparked a

---

[34] European Union External Action (2021).

question about possible alignment or cooperation with this body. In response, the Dutch government stated that it is open to explore cooperation "with the Quad and individual Quad members at EU-level."

This suggests that the tactics of European governments in implementing their Indo-Pacific strategies should be in relation to the Quad, and therefore the United States. While this may have its advantages, it may also have its drawbacks. ASEAN countries and India generally wish for the EU's Indo-Pacific actions to be independent, and some EU member states, especially France, will still desire autonomy from the American approach. France is unlikely to want to follow America's lead in the Quad or other arrangements, especially after the fallout from the AUKUS announcement. Although France will cooperate with the United States and likely prioritize that cooperation, France will still want to continue acting independently and autonomously from the United States. There are already signs of this as France has moved forward on improving strategic partnerships with Australia, India and Japan.

Against this context, the EU would do well to align with but not to get on board with the Quad. Also, cooperation is more likely at the EU level—rather than at the level of EU member states—as the EU Indo-Pacific strategy states that it is interested in engaging with the Quad on issues of common interest, such as climate change, technology or vaccines. However, beyond these areas there are no further hints at cooperation within the document. On the other hand, the leaders of the Quad countries did publicly welcome the EU strategy[35] during the first ever, in-person Quad summit held in September, 2021. Despite some willingness on both sides, it may be too early to tell what EU-Quad cooperation will look like in the near future. Non-security issues, especially climate change and vaccines, are likely to be the prioritizations since they are largely uncontroversial and non-political.

Despite NATO being increasingly concerned with China as an opponent, a NATO presence in the Indo-Pacific is not under consideration in European circles. Nor is it desirable to Indo-Pacific countries, as this would seriously antagonise China. However, with a view to implementing the connectivity agenda, there are benefits to the EU linking to NATO partnerships in the region. In recent years, NATO has strengthened relationships with New Zealand, South Korea, Japan, and Australia in particular. These newly reinforced relationships could be beneficial to the EU. Again, the digital realm should be especially considered. The NATO Cyber Cooperative Cyber Defence Centre of Excellence is developing closer relations with these four countries.[36] Existing efforts of individual EU member states, such as that of the Netherlands Defence Cyber Command, complement this. Within NATO itself there is currently some debate on whether more out-of-area (OOA) missions should be undertaken. Before cooperation with the EU in the Indo-Pacific can be undertaken,

---

[35] "The Quad" leaders present united front at White House. (2021) *Deutsche Welle*. https://www.dw.com/en/the-quad-summit-indo-pacific-leaders-present-united-front/a-59299599. Accessed April 2023.

[36] North Atlantic Treaty Organization (2023).

NATO must first make up its own mind on how it will contribute to security in the region.

Ultimately the EU has options in the Indo-Pacific and can adjust depending on what avenues its member states deem most appropriate. On one hand, the EU has the lead in putting forward a coordinated approach—bringing key stakeholders together in what is increasingly more often called a "Team Europe" approach. On the other, individual member states engage with the region and focus on niche areas where each of them can be most effective and successful, while remaining committed to the general guidelines within the EU Connectivity and EU Indo-Pacific Strategies. A coalition of the willing EU member states may also be the best, as some states are more interested in Indo-Pacific engagement than others and may not be willing to expend resources on a region which does not benefit their interests.

Divergences and Convergences on the LIO in Europe and "The West"

Although most Western countries have given some credence to the need to strengthen the LIO or rules-based international order, the individual conceptualizations and policy approaches to the world order vary. This section discusses the four main challenges that academics and policymakers face when adopting the concept of the liberal international order as an analytical lens in discussions on Europe's newfound connectivity activism in the Indo-Pacific.

What (Element of the) LIO Is Addressed?

First, although rarely discussed in such terms, the EU connectivity agenda and key elements in the EU's recent turn to the Indo-Pacific seek to defend, update and promote different versions of the liberal international order (LIO) as identified by Hans Kundnani.[37] The connectivity agenda seeks primarily to promote European interests in the liberal economic order as well as the political liberal order. Moving beyond the globalization and openness that characterized the liberal economic order earlier, the EU connectivity agenda now seeks to promote openness, conditional globalization—based on sustainability and high-quality—next to targeted defensive policies that are tied to the EU's rethink on industrial policy including more diversified supply chains and investment screening. Separately, and more specifically, the EU's push in the digital/cyber domain in the Indo-Pacific is primarily about defending updating key elements of the economic liberal order and promoting core principles of the political liberal order, in which the concepts of democracy, human-centered and rules-based systems take more prominence, next to openness. Lastly, the EU's

---

[37] See the concluding chapter of this book.

activism in the Indo-Pacific maritime domain primarily relates the liberal order as an IR-concept (concept of international relations), wherein state sovereignty is central. Compared to the other two elements, the EU's approach has changed less as the aim is still for a rules-based LIO.

A key point to note is that the EU and its member states and Japan share more between them than each of them shares with the U.S., which is less willing to accept the rules-based IR-LIO in the maritime domain (as may be derived from the fact that it is not a member of UNCLOS) and less willing to join a political rules-based LIO 2.0 in the digital domain (and instead, more willing to go-it-alone while pressuring partners to join its bandwagon). That said, neither the EU nor Japan is able—or really willing—to hold the U.S. more accountable in a LIO 2.0, as both still rely on the U.S. security guarantees. Yet, the EU and Japan are challenged in their position to the extent to which they—and other countries—consider U.S. actions to be a positive contribution to global public goods (e.g., international security and stability, freedom of navigation, free trade, financial stability) while their opposition to (elements of) its ideological underpinnings grows.

Industrial Policies Undermining the LIO?

Second, we are witnessing a profound change in approach to economic policies. This is evident from the international connectivity agenda, as from the turn to new domestic (or: EU-internal) industrial policies. The typical neo-liberal approach which has categorized liberal democracies since the 1980s is giving way to a new economic status quo. The often times blind devotion to allowing the free market to drive the economic route a country takes, is being replaced by a new willingness of governments to intervene in the economy. While this shift is not necessarily a threat to the LIO, it is a significant global trend which must be accounted for.

There are various causes for this shift in economic policies. A leading cause is the "clash of capitalisms" that is increasingly evident, as neo-liberal market economies are having to compete with a state capitalist country. This has exposed the weaknesses of the West's market-driven approach, as private companies struggle to compete with (state and private companies) that receive financial and more indirect support from the state. Closely intertwined in this growing apprehension is the "free riding" issue: the idea that there are countries, especially China, that make use of the benefits of open, transparent economics, but do not adhere to these ideals themselves. Worries that the West cannot keep up with China's economic growth are also encouraging policymakers to intervene economically, especially in strategic and high-tech sectors of the economy where they do not want to be overly dependent on non-market players.

Complementing this challenge at the global level, domestically, Western economies are now grappling with the impact of de-industrialization, the outsourcing of manufacturing jobs and other negative trends which governments are increasingly aiming to halt or reverse. The economic challenges have led to societal issues such as the rise of populism, political polarization and general discontent among the greater public. Finally, COVID-19 had a significant role in completing the shift towards more industrial policies, with the rapid normalization of historically large stimulus funds being utilized to address the economic fallout of the pandemic.

For these and other reasons, cracks in neo-liberalism are beginning to show. In the United States, one of the firmest supporters of the free market, the shift towards economic intervention became particularly evident under former President Trump. U.S. policies were openly protectionist, and even turned against allies in Europe and in Asia. But also under President Biden, national security concerns are, in the views of Europeans at least, used as a guise for protectionist economic policies. Illustrative of the break[38] from America's previous economic status quo, the U.S. Innovation and Competition Act—a piece of legislation intended to directly address the America's waning competitiveness with China—was passed in June of 2021 with rare bipartisan support.[39]

The policies of European governments and businesses in the trade, high-tech, and digital domains especially are undergoing profound changes. Countries across the world are now increasingly willing to see the return of industrial policies, protectionism, capital controls, macroprudential regulation and state capitalism. Economic anxiety is changing the perception of policymakers, but also of corporations. Stakeholders have a growing awareness and willingness to act to mitigate geopolitical risks, in particular concerning China. Throughout Western societies there is a growing understanding that contemporary economic challenges cannot be solved with the previous neo-liberal approach. However, most European policymakers want to uphold the architecture of the global economic system; they still believe that an update of the basic principles of the rules-based system will suffice.

Can We Connect the Dots?

Third, one of the key characteristics that is both a push factor and a consequence of the breakdown of the liberal international order, is that the various elements of the LIO that governments attempted to keep separate in the post-1945 period—when the LIO was (re)shaped by Western countries—are increasingly interlinked. For example, while NATO used to address "just" security issues on the European continent, it now also deals with cyber-attacks allegedly originating in China on Western companies. And human rights are today increasingly considered in the trade and security realms, for example in exports of cotton from Xinjiang and in export controls of dual-use

---

[38] Biden Just Gave the Most Ideologically Ambitious Speech of Any Democratic President in Generations. (2021) *Politico*. https://www.politico.com/news/magazine/2021/04/29/biden-speech-ideologically-ambitious-484990/. Accessed April 2023.

[39] What's in the China competitiveness bill? (2021) *CNN*. https://edition.cnn.com/2021/06/08/politics/china-innovation-competition-bill-explainer/index.html/. Accessed April 2023.

items such as surveillance cameras. In the words of Sabine Weyand, EU Director-General for Trade: "We can no longer separate international economic policy from foreign policy," and adding "This is more difficult for the EU than for others."[40]

The connectivity agenda may be the clearest example of the need to break the silos between policy fields and the challenge of the EU in doing so. After all, connectivity is concerned with a variety of policy domains—including trade, transport, energy, digital and foreign affairs—and is also informed by (non-traditional) security concerns. It is therefore problematic to conceive the evolving LIO still in traditional terms, as this widens the disconnect between academic debates and the real world wherein such distinctions are blurred. In fact, doing so reinforces the challenge that many Western experts (much like policymakers) face in fundamentally rethinking the emerging existing order and appropriate policies to adapt to it in order to pursue our interests.

Some countries, including the United States and Japan, tackled this challenge of whole-of-government coordination on economic security issues by creating a National Security Council (or similar agency) already years ago. In the EU there were similar calls to "connect the dots," but it took the Covid-19 crisis to get to greater coordination—between EU institutions and with EU member states, both in Brussels and in European operations in third countries. While the so-called "Team Europe approach" was first applied to vaccines and health policy more generally, it expanded to other policy areas also—including China policy. So-called Team Europe Initiatives (TEIs) are now implemented in developing countries, especially in the European neighborhood. These offer a valuable template also for future connectivity projects in other regions.

What Are (Hidden) Differences Between Rhetorical Devices and Conceptualizations?

Fourth, it is clear from the rhetorical devices and concepts employed that countries differ in their approaches to the LIO, even within Europe. Notably, none of the official EU documents for connectivity and the Indo-Pacific include any direct reference to "liberal" or the liberal international order. But while the European approach to connectivity, including in the Indo-Pacific, is inclusive, it is not value-neutral. The EU Indo-Pacific strategy, like the Dutch Guidelines, calls for effective rules-based multilateralism and is generally inclusive in tone. But approaches and specific actions of EU member states show clear preferences for collaborating with like-minded partners. Democratic countries with free markets will be prioritized as the EU is eager to help uphold liberal values and norms in a region in which they are increasingly being contested.

---

[40] Brugel (2021).

Clearly, countries vary on which key rhetorical devices and conceptualizations are utilized and emphasized as they redefine their foreign policies in a changing LIO. Three distinctions stand out and will be directly addressed here.

First, some countries prefer to emphasize cooperation between "like-minded countries" over countries that share interests or concerns, and the style of cooperation may vary depending on whether the partner countries is either "like-minded" or has "shared interests." The Dutch Indo-Pacific Guidelines for example call for closer cooperation with like-minded democracies and countries with open market economies, stating that "partnerships will take different forms in different countries depending on the extent of shared interests and the degree of like-mindedness." The Council's conclusions on connectivity state that this "renewed commitment to the region is inclusive of all partners wishing to cooperate with the EU," and that the EU is to "build its cooperation according to specific policy areas where partners can find common ground based on shared principles, values or mutual interest." This is an important distinction to consider because European policy will need to walk a fine line between maintaining ties with troubled democracies while not rewarding authoritarian behavior. On the other hand, acting too harshly towards these states may cause them to double down on authoritarianism, and move closer to China.

Second, the idea of a democratic alliance[41]—whether it is referred to as the D10, summit of democracies or another name—has been floated by a number of world leaders, including President Biden and British Prime Minister Boris Johnson. In the EU, while no reference to "democracy" or "democratic" is included in the 2018 connectivity strategy, the various documents released in 2021 reference "democracy" more than "rules-based."

However, the rhetorical turn to democratic values needs to be scrutinized with a view to the fact that democracy has been under pressure also in the United States and various European countries. Moreover, creating yet another multilateral format may not be the solution. While an alliance dedicated explicitly to upholding liberal values and democracy sounds attractive, it may not be practical. The formation of such an alliance is sure to be somewhat contentious as a decision will need to be made on whether the alliance is inclusive or exclusive, meaning whether weak or seriously flawed democracies, or authoritarian states under the guise of democracy will be included. The effectiveness is also potentially difficult since democracies are themselves very diverse and have far ranging interests.

Lastly, the focus on rules-based multilateralism, which Germany has highlighted, should be contrasted with a focus on a rules-based order, the approach France has emphasized. This distinction between EU member states will explore whether the difference is just in rhetoric or a preference to use one's state's strong suit in practice. These differences in conceptualization are necessarily to reflect upon, as they speak volumes about each state's approach to the LIO.

Analyzing the differing approaches to the Indo-Pacific region is a suitable case study by which an understanding of the two most influential EU member states' foreign policy posture can be formulated. Germany has tended to prefer a "rules-based

---

[41] White House (2021b).

multilateralism" approach, as evidenced by the contents of the German Indo-Pacific Guidelines. This approach shies away from direct strategic partnership generally and prefers to work through existing multilateral frameworks. There are exceptions, but generally multilateralism is preferred by the German government. The guidelines put special emphasis on engaging with multilateral frameworks such as ASEAN more than pursuing greater and deeper strategic partnerships with individual countries. The document emphasizes the centrality of ASEAN in Germany's push to be more active in security issues in the Indo-Pacific. For example, rather than unilateral or bilateral actions to ensure the South China Sea remains secure and open for maritime trade, Germany is pushing for increased dialogue between ASEAN and China to establish a sustainable code of conduct for the disputed sea. In addition, there is also a preference for using diplomatic or economic tools to secure interests in the Indo-Pacific, before resorting to other means.

France, however, has taken a different stance. Rather than multilateralism, France has tended to favor supporting the rules-based order through primarily focusing on the enforcement, through bilateral and trilateral partnerships, of central aspects of that world order. France sees itself, not only as a partner of the Indo-Pacific, but as an Indo-Pacific country in its own right due to its territories in the region. Therefore, France's approaches to the Indo-Pacific were conceived to defend its sovereignty and control over the French Indo-Pacific possessions. For this reason, much more of the French Indo-Pacific strategy is dedicated to military preparedness and security cooperation than Germany's. Furthermore, the French government is prioritizing strategic partnerships with countries such as Australia, India and Japan, rather than multilateral formats. However, although this preference is clearly signalled, the French document does include cooperation with ASEAN and other multilateral frameworks as necessary tools to addressing the tensions in the region.

Although the French and German approaches vary somewhat, it is clear that both states are increasingly concerned with the fracturing international order. However, a clear difference between the EU member states and the U.K. can be seen. While the U.K. is readying itself and anticipating a shift from the current international status quo to some new form of world order, France and Germany seem to have remained committed to maintaining and reinforcing the current international order. Although the international shifts, especially the intensifying rivalry between the United States and China, are putting tremendous strain on the norms and values of the current international order, France and Germany remain optimistic enough to believe that the order is not beyond saving.

Conclusion

The EU connectivity Agenda, now rebranded as the Global Gateway, can be seen as the EU's indirect response to two of the most pressing international shifts since the end of the Cold War. First, the connectivity agenda is meant to address the challenge of a rising China, especially China's bid to increase its influence through the BRI.

The Global Gateway is set to give target states of the BRI a safer bet which will still meet the infrastructure needs of states in the region. The Global Gateway is set to develop infrastructure projects, both traditional and non-traditional, which are environmentally and financially sustainable. These projects will not only have a positive economic impact for both Europe and its partners, but they will also help to reinforce democratic and liberal values within these partner countries by presenting an alternative to Chinese investment and by addressing the needs of the public, thereby winning popular support. For this latter aspect, a strong, driving narrative is essential for the EU's success.

Therefore, while the Global Gateway indirectly contends with China's global outreach through the BRI, it also indirectly addresses the increasingly worrying strain on the LIO. By maintaining an emphasis on sustainability and, more recently, emphasizing trusted connectivity, the EU can combine economic growth with strengthened liberal values. The inclusion of regulatory aspects in the Global Gateway will also be important in this process, as these regulations, especially in the digital domain, will have democratic values integrated within them which directly challenge the digital authoritarianism of China. Especially in the Indo-Pacific, a region where the EU increasingly wants to assert itself, this policy agenda is of vital importance to maintaining and improving the EU's global economic competitiveness and strategic advantages.

Whether the EU can be successful in implementing this agenda in the Indo-Pacific will depend on its ability to work with partners in the region and with the United States. Clearly, it is not realistic to expect the EU to be able to do this on its own. While strategic ambiguity may at times be a valuable asset, clarity about concepts, developing potential to deliver on those—including thorough integrated approaches—as well as critical self-reflection on how domestic strategic adjustments may be perceived by others as undermining the LIO, are needed as the EU moves from strategy to implementation with its connectivity agenda in the Indo-Pacific.

References

Associated Press. (2021). Harris calls on Vietnam to join in opposing China "bullying," *Politico*. Retrieved April 2023, from https://www.politico.com/news/2021/08/25/kamala-harris-vietnam-china-506863

Brugel. (2021). *Navigating a more polarized world: Policy implications*. Retrieved April 2023, from https://www.bruegel.org/event/navigating-more-polarised-world-policy-implications/

Dekker, B., Chan, H., & Okano-Hejimans, M. (2022). Growing stronger together: Towards and EU-ASEAN Digital Partnership? *Clingendael Report*. Clingendael Institute.

Escober, P. (2020). China rolls out the Health Silk Road, *Asia Times*. Retrieved April 2023, from https://asiatimes.com/2020/04/china-rolls-out-the-health-silk-road/

European Commission. (2019a). *Global Gateway*. Retrieved April 2023, from https://commission.europa.eu/strategy-and-policy/priorities-2019-2024/stronger-europe-world/global-gateway_en

European Commission. (2019b). *EU-China strategic outlook: Commission and HR/VP contribution to the European Council* (March 21–22, 2019). Retrieved April 2023, from https://commission.europa.eu/publications/eu-china-strategic-outlook-commission-and-hrvp-contribution-european-council-21-22-march-2019_en

European Commission. (2020). *Joint communication: A new EU-US agenda for global change*. Retrieved April 2023, from https://commission.europa.eu/document/da473743-1205-45c3-a558-87d0bf356cbd_en

European Commission. (2021a). *2021 State of the union address by President von der Leyen*. Retrieved April 2023, from https://ec.europa.eu/commission/presscorner/detail/en/SPEECH_21_4701

European Commission. (2021b). *State of the Union 2021*. Retrieved April 2023, from https://state-of-the-union.ec.europa.eu/state-union-2021_en

European Commission. (2021c). *Questions and answers: EU strategy for cooperation in the Indo-Pacific*. Retrieved April 2023, from https://ec.europa.eu/commission/presscorner/detail/en/qanda_21_4709

European Commission. (2022). *The twin green & digital transition: How sustainable digital technologies could enable a carbon-neutral EU by 2050*. Retrieved April 2023, from https://joint-research-centre.ec.europa.eu/jrc-news/twin-green-digital-transition-how-sustainable-digital-technologies-could-enable-carbon-neutral-eu-2022-06-29_en

European Council of European Union. (2021a). *A globally connected Europe: Council approves conclusions*. Retrieved April 2023, from https://www.consilium.europa.eu/en/press/press-releases/2021/07/12/a-globally-connected-europe-council-approves-conclusions/

European Council of European Union. (2021b). "EU's Digital Revolution: fueling our connectivity strategy"—Keynote speech by President Charles Michel at the Tallinn Digital Summit. Retrieved April 2023, from https://www.consilium.europa.eu/en/press/press-releases/2021/09/07/keynote-speech-by-president-charles-michel-at-the-tallinn-digital-summit/

European Council of European Union. (2021c). EU-India leaders' meeting via video conference, *Porto* (May 8, 2021). Retrieved April 2023, from https://www.consilium.europa.eu/en/meetings/international-summit/2021/05/08/?utm_source=twitter.com&utm_medium=social&utm_campaign=2021-05-08-eu-india-leaders-meeting&utm_content=video

European Parliament. (2021a). *Chinese counter-sanctions on EU targets*. Retrieved April 2023, from https://www.europarl.europa.eu/thinktank/en/document/EPRS_ATA(2021)690617

European Parliament. (2021b). *European Parliament resolution of 21 January 2021 on connectivity and EU-Asia relations*. Retrieved April 2023, from https://www.europarl.europa.eu/doceo/document/TA-9-2021-0016_EN.html

European Union External Action. (2021). *United States: High representative/Vice President Josep Borrell met with Secretary of State Antony Blinken*. Retrieved April 2023, from https://www.eeas.europa.eu/eeas/united-states-high-representativevice-president-josep-borrell-met-secretary-state-antony-0_en/

Government of Netherlands. (2020). *Indo-Pacific: Guidelines for strengthening Dutch and EU cooperation with partners in Asia*. Retrieved April 2023, from https://www.government.nl/documents/publications/2020/11/13/indo-pacific-guidelines

John, W. (2021). China's innovation dilemma, *The Interpreter*. Retrieved April 2023, from https://www.lowyinstitute.org/the-interpreter/china-s-innovation-dilemma

Kurlantzick, J., & West, J. (2020). *Council on foreign relations*. Retrieved April 2023, from https://www.cfr.org/china-digital-silk-road/?gclid=CjwKCAjwmqKJBhAWEiwAMvGt6BfAA8Wzu1C2eG9mLGPb6HJYxxACxSmjlsuLpFqgoWTRUKBJuGrGcBoCxXAQAvD_BwE

Lau, S., & Cokelaere, H. (2021). EU launches "Global Gateway" to counter China's Belt and Road, *Politico*. https://www.politico.eu/article/eu-launches-global-gateway-to-counter-chinas-belt-and-road/

Maaike, O.-H., & Tomoki, K. (2019). *Engaging but not endorsing China's Belt and Road Initiative*, Netherlands Institute of International Relations. Retrieved April 2023, from https://www.clingendael.org/sites/default/files/2019-05/PB_China_Belt_and_Road_Initiative_May_2019.pdf

Marc, A., Norbert, R., & Margriet, V. (2021). EU's Indo-Pacific strategy stands ready to deepen EU-Asean ties, *The Business Times*. Retrieved April 2023, from https://www.businesstimes.com.sg/international/eus-indo-pacific-strategy-stands-ready-deepen-eu-asean-ties

Ministry of Foreign Affairs of Japan. (2015). *Announcement of "Partnership for Quality Infrastructure: Investment for Asia's Future."* Retrieved April 2023, from https://www.mofa.go.jp/policy/oda/page18_000076.html

North Atlantic Treaty Organization. (2023). *Relations with partners in the Indo Pacific region*. Retrieved April 2023, from https://www.nato.int/cps/en/natohq/topics_183254.htm

Okano-Heijmans, M. (2023). Open strategic autonomy: The digital dimension. *Clingendael Report*. Clingendael Institute.

Okano-Heijmans, M., & Shah, V. (2022). Multistakeholderism: The path to human-centered digital connectivity. *AESCON Policy Brief Series* 2022-01.

Sophie, T. (2017). Trump defends Putin: "You think our country's so innocent?" *CNN Politics*. Retrieved April 2023, from https://edition.cnn.com/2017/02/04/politics/donald-trump-vladimir-putin/index.html

Steve, H., & Michael, H. (2021). G7 rivals China with grand infrastructure plan, *Reuters*. Retrieved April 2023, from https://www.reuters.com/world/g7-counter-chinas-belt-road-with-infrastructure-project-senior-us-official-2021-06-12/

The Diplomatic Service of European Union. (2019). *Connecting Europe & Asia: The EU Strategy*. Retrieved April 2023, from https://www.eeas.europa.eu/eeas/connecting-europe-asia-eu-strategy_en

The European External Action Service. (2019). *The partnership on sustainable connectivity and quality infrastructure between the European Union and Japan*. Retrieved April 2023, from https://www.eeas.europa.eu/eeas/partnership-sustainable-connectivity-and-quality-infrastructure-between-european-union-and_en

U.S. Department of State. (2021). *Secretary Antony J. Blinken, National Security Advisor Jake Sullivan, Director Yang and State Councilor Wang at the top of their meeting*. Retrieved April 2023, from https://www.state.gov/secretary-antony-j-blinken-national-security-advisor-jake-sullivan-chinese-director-of-the-office-of-the-central-commission-for-foreign-affairs-yang-jie chi-and-chinese-state-councilor-wang-yi-at-th/

White House. (2021a). *Remarks by Vice President Harris at the United States Naval academy graduation and commissioning ceremony*. Retrieved April 2023, from https://www.whitehouse.gov/briefing-room/speeches-remarks/2021/05/28/remarks-by-vice-president-harris-at-the-united-states-naval-academy-graduation-and-commissioning-ceremony/

White House. (2021b). *President Biden to convene leader's summit for democracy*. Retrieved April 2023, from https://www.whitehouse.gov/briefing-room/statements-releases/2021/08/11/president-biden-to-convene-leaders-summit-for-democracy/

Open Access This chapter is licensed under the terms of the Creative Commons Attribution-NonCommercial-NoDerivatives 4.0 International License (http://creativecommons.org/licenses/by-nc-nd/4.0/), which permits any noncommercial use, sharing, distribution and reproduction in any medium or format, as long as you give appropriate credit to the original author(s) and the source, provide a link to the Creative Commons license and indicate if you modified the licensed material. You do not have permission under this license to share adapted material derived from this chapter or parts of it.

The images or other third party material in this chapter are included in the chapter's Creative Commons license, unless indicated otherwise in a credit line to the material. If material is not included in the chapter's Creative Commons license and your intended use is not permitted by statutory regulation or exceeds the permitted use, you will need to obtain permission directly from the copyright holder.

Chapter 5
Germany's Indo-Pacific Turn: Towards a Contribution to the Rules-Based Order?

Alexandra Sakaki

Abstract Germany has shown significant interest in the Indo-Pacific region since around 2020, when it published policy guidelines focused on this region. In that context, one of Berlin's professed objectives has been to contribute to the rules-based international order. Whereas its policy was dominated by economic and trade issues in the past, Berlin has shifted more attention to security issues. The deployment of a frigate to the Indo-Pacific in 2021–2022 underlined the Federal Republic's growing interest in the region, although it is questionable as to what extent it contributed to the rules-based order. Germany's Indo-Pacific policy goes beyond this deployment, however, covering a broad range of issues encapsulated by a whole-of-government approach. Disaggregating the concept of liberal international order into the three major elements—security order, economic order, and human rights order—this chapter shows that Germany's policy reflects support for all three dimensions in the region. Nevertheless, Berlin will need continued refinement of its approach, such as determining the extent of policy cooperation with Washington or engagement with minilateral frameworks in the region.

European interest in the Indo-Pacific has grown over recent years, with Germany among the countries at the forefront of this trend. The Federal Republic was the second European country after France to issue policy guidelines on this region in September 2020, two months before the Netherlands followed suit. Those three countries furthermore served as driving forces behind the process that led to the announcement of the European Union's Indo-Pacific Strategy in September 2021. As a sign of its growing engagement, the Federal Republic deployed a frigate to the region between August 2021 and February 2022, the first time in almost two decades that one of its warship cruised the Indo-Pacific. In the summer of 2022, the German Air Force also deployed to the Indo-Pacific, taking part in multinational exercises in Australia.

A. Sakaki (✉)
Deputy Head of Asia Division, German Institute for International and Security Affairs (Stiftung Wissenschaft Und Politik, SWP), Berlin, Germany

© The International House of Japan, Inc. 2024
Y. Hosoya and H. Kundnani (eds.), *The Transformation of the Liberal International Order*, SpringerBriefs in International Relations,
https://doi.org/10.1007/978-981-99-4729-4_5

In this context, one of the professed objectives of German policy in the region is to contribute to the rules-based order founded on multilateral cooperation and international law, reflecting a realization that the existing order is increasingly weakened and imperiled. The Indo-Pacific deserves particular attention as the decisive region where "the shape of tomorrow's international order will be decided," according to then-Foreign Minister Heiko Maas in the September 2020 policy guidelines.[1]

The Federal Republic undoubtedly has a strong incentive to defend the existing liberal international order, on which its post-war freedom and prosperity have depended. Against that background, a number of academics have voiced expectations in recent years for Germany—along with Japan as another major beneficiary of the existing order—to contribute more to upholding the central features of that order, especially as U.S. willingness to serve as the bedrock of liberal internationalism has weakened.[2] To avoid alienating countries that are unsupportive of liberal norms such as democracy or human rights, German decision-makers and policy documents generally employ the term rules-based order rather than liberal international order.

This contribution provides an overview of Germany's Indo-Pacific policy turn and its characteristics, assessing the extent to which the country has shown an inclination to contribute to the rules-based order. It also considers the sustainability of German engagement, reflecting the impact of the change in Federal government in December 2021 and the Russian invasion of Ukraine launched in February 2022.

Shifting Interest in the Indo-Pacific

Identifying itself as a continental power focused on Europe, Germany has for long viewed the Indo-Pacific region from a somewhat detached position. By comparison, France and the United Kingdom have deeper historical links as well as overseas territories that shape their respective approaches.[3] At least until recently, Germany pursued mainly economic opportunities in this region, whereas political and security-related issues did not feature high on the agenda. This one-sided pursuit of commercial interests was epitomized by Chancellor Angela Merkel's China policy between 2005 and 2021, when Berlin appeared slow to adapt to Beijing's growing international assertiveness and authoritarianism, especially under President Xi Jinping.

Nevertheless, towards the end of Merkel's chancellorship, German optimism about China eroded noticeably in light of Beijing's human rights abuses, its "wolf warrior" diplomacy and disinformation campaigns, as well as its open dismissal of international rules as happened after the 2016 South China Sea arbitration ruling. Chinese international conduct increasingly cast doubts about the long-standing notion in German foreign policy of "Wandel durch Handel" or "change through

---

[1] Federal Government/Foreign Ministry (2020).

[2] Ikenberry (2022), Krauss and Maull (2020), Daalder and Linsdsay (2018).

[3] On France and U.K., see for example, Nouwens and Mohan (2021). See also Céline Pajon's contribution in this volume.

trade," which was based on the assumption that authoritarian regimes can be socialized into the existing order through economic engagement that would lead to political transformation. That expectation was fully discredited by Russia's invasion of Ukraine in February 2022.[4]

The publication of Germany's Indo-Pacific guidelines signified a reevaluation of the importance of the entire region. The document seeks to formulates a more holistic approach to the unfolding dynamics across policy areas, shifting attention away from China by diversifying and deepening relations with other partners in the region. Given that the Federal Republic conducts about 20 percent of its total trade in goods with the region, it has a paramount interest in preserving peace and stability.[5] Beyond economic considerations, Germany's shifting attention to the Indo-Pacific signifies an acknowledgement of the challenges posed to the existing rules-based order by China's international assertiveness. At the same time, Berlin is concerned about the deepening Sino-American rivalry, fearing the emergence of bipolarity with sharp dividing lines that will undermine prospects for global economic and political cooperation, leading to a fragmented world order.

Botched Start: Germany's Indo-Pacific Deployment in 2021–2022

The Indo-Pacific deployment of the frigate "Bayern" in 2021–22 was the first clear signal of German presence and interest in the region following the guidelines' publication. As a training and presence mission that did not require a parliamentary mandate, the voyage was primarily political in nature. The ship's voyage was intended to revive Germany's relationships in the region and provide impetus for closer military and diplomatic consultations. On this count, the deployment was successful. Another objective, however, was to contribute to the maintenance of the rules-based international order.[6] The mission only did justice to that aspiration to a limited extent.

The Federal Government repeatedly cited the frigate's role in monitoring United Nations sanctions against North Korea as a concrete contribution to order in the region. According to insiders, the frigate indeed successfully collected information on the activities of a number of ships, reporting these to the Enforcement Coordination Cell (ECC) in Japan, which coordinates the monitoring of UN sanctions.[7] Nevertheless, sanctions monitoring was likely not the top priority for the entire period of four weeks in which the German ship officially contributed to the mission, as it also took part in a large-scale drill called "Annual Exercise 2021," hosted by Japan in

---

[4] Lars Klingbeil, co-leader of the Social Democratic Party, that is at the forefront of the three-party coalition government under Olaf Scholz, declared in April 2022 that this notion had failed. See Kinkartz (2022)

[5] Federal Government/Foreign Ministry, "Policy Guidelines for the Indo-Pacific," 9.

[6] See for example, Federal Foreign Ministry (2022).

[7] Interview with insider in Tokyo, November 2022.

the Philippine Sea, and made a port call in South Korea during this time. Therefore, it is unclear how extensive the operative benefit of the frigate's information collection was for the UN surveillance mission.

The Federal Republic also failed to take a clear stance on China's extensive maritime claims in the South China Sea, which Berlin had previously rejected with reference to international law. In traversing the South China Sea, the Bayern stayed on the common international shipping routes and refrained (as far as is publicly known) from any military drills, such as helicopter take-off and landing. This conduct could even be read as recognizing Chinese claims. According to the UN Convention on the Law of the Sea (UNCLOS), merchant ships and warships only have the right to "innocent passage" through other countries' territorial seas. They must move along the shortest routes—and thus along the common trade routes—and warships must not carry out military exercises. By contrast, ships at high sea have almost unlimited freedom of movement and are allowed to hold drills. By sticking to the narrow code of conduct of "innocent passage'," the German ship missed the chance to take a clear stand against China's illegal territorial claims.

Initially, the plan had been for the frigate to make a port call in Shanghai. Had this happened, Germany's position would have appeared even less clear.[8] A stop in China before the Bayern's passage through the South China Sea would have looked like a request for permission and thus reinforced the perception that Germany respects Beijing's claims. The purpose of the proposed visit, according to then Defense Minister Annegret Kramp-Karrenbauer, had been to keep dialogue open with China, in line with Germany's "inclusive" approach, which seeks to engage all actors.[9] In the end, however, the Chinese leadership rejected the port call, pointing to a lack of trust between the two countries.

Beyond the Frigate: Contributing to the Rules-Based Order

The frigate's deployment highlighted a need for Germany to reflect and refine its approach in order to make a meaningful contribution to the rules-based order in the Indo-Pacific. For the government of Chancellor Olaf Scholz, which came into office in December 2021, the policy guidelines on the Indo-Pacific continue to serve as orientation. This was underlined in the federal government's two-year progress report on Indo-Pacific policy issued in September 2022, which explicitly "reaffirms" the policy guidelines.[10] That report also underlined Germany's goal to "preserve the rules-based international order, strengthen international law and multilateral structures and prevent conflicts." Since the first publication of Indo-Pacific Policy Guidelines, Berlin has overall made a strong push to diversify its relations with regional countries

---

[8] See also Kundnani and Tsuruoka (2021).

[9] Federal Ministry of Defense (2022).

[10] See Federal Government of Germany (2022).

other than China, for example by pursuing new consultation formats, engaging with more frequent high-level visits, or initiating concrete cooperation.

Representing a whole-of-government approach, the guidelines comprehensively cover various policy fields and thus offer insights into Germany's engagement beyond the frigate's deployment. If one disaggregates the concept of liberal international order into the three major elements, that is, security order, economic order and human rights order, then German policy reflects support for all three dimensions in the Indo-Pacific.[11]

In the security area, Germany has and will continue to contribute through rhetorical backing for international rules and principles. Berlin has already supported critical statements on China's conduct in the South and East China Seas in the G7 framework as well as in a joint note verbale to the UN in September 2020 together with France and the U.K. The Federal Republic also pursues some small-scale projects in the area of security, such as training ministerial staff and government officials in Southeast Asia and South Asia on the interpretation and implementation of UNCLOS. Furthermore, Germany started a pilot project with the Philippine coastguard in June 2022 to improve the country's maritime resilience by providing two reconnaissance drones and relevant training for operators.[12]

Despite thinly stretched military resources after decades of fiscal austerity, Germany is also making efforts to deploy Bundeswehr assets to the region more regularly. In its Air Force deployment in 2022, Berlin sent six Eurofighters and seven other transport and tanker aircraft to the Indo-Pacific, taking part in two Australian multilateral exercises called Pitch Black and Kakadu.[13] According to the Inspector of the Air Force Ingo Gerhartz, Germany sought to demonstrate that it could fulfill its alliance commitments on NATO's eastern flank amid the Russian war on Ukraine, while simultaneously mobilizing aircraft to the Indo-Pacific within less than 24 h.[14] Germany is also making plans for further deployments to the region by the Ground Forces in 2023 and by the Maritime forces in 2024. The main purpose is to deepen security cooperation with regional partners and foster interoperability, thereby signaling the importance Germany attaches to the region. Privately, officials also admit that Germany seeks to contribute to deterring China from actions that would destabilize the region.[15] Overall, Germany will still have to continue to weigh deployments to the Indo-Pacific carefully, given that the Russian war on Ukraine demands a concentration of resources in Europe.[16]

---

[11] On the three dimensions, also see Kundnani (2017).

[12] Federal Government of Germany (2022).

[13] For further details, see Bundeswehr (2022).

[14] Ingo Gerhartz called this ability to mobilize in two region the new "level of ambition" that Germany has after the "Zeitenwende" or change of era, that was proclaimed by Chancellor Olaf Scholz in February 2022. See Gerhartz (2022).

[15] Personal conversations with security-related officials, November 2022.

[16] The increased funding for the Bundeswehr announced by Chancellor Scholz in February 2022 will have an impact in the medium term at the earliest.

In the economic area, the EU is in the lead as it has exclusive competence in trade matters. Nevertheless, German support for EU negotiations in pursuit of free trade agreements (FTAs) in the Indo-Pacific region is important, given the country's status as the largest economy of the bloc and Berlin's close political ties with the European Commission's trade negotiation team.[17] Berlin sees the EU's high-quality trade agreements with Japan, New Zealand, South Korea, Singapore and Vietnam as important tools to stand up for the principle of free trade, to codify rules and standards, and to resist protectionism, while also providing a means to reduce dependencies on products from a single market. Therefore, it "strongly supports the European Union's proactive trade policy, which aims to strengthen the multilateral trade system with the WTO at its center," according to the Indo-Pacific policy guidelines.[18] The two-year progress report on Indo-Pacific policy in September 2022 specifically mentioned Berlin's support for negotiations by the European Commission for FTAs with Australia, India and Indonesia. Nevertheless, German officials also admit that such negotiations by the EU can be cumbersome and time-consuming, and therefore more pragmatism may be required on Europe's part to ensure continued progress in some cases.[19] Germany also supports the EU's initiatives to foster connectivity and develop infrastructure in the Indo-Pacific, seeing it as another tool to promote coherent regulations, standards and procedures.

Germany's push for the finalization of the EU's long-delayed Comprehensive Agreement on Investment (CAI) with China in December 2020 during its EU Council presidency was controversial, however. Proponents of the agreement argued that it would help increase legal certainty, improve market access and establish fair conditions for engagement by European companies, effectively binding China more closely to a rules-based trade order.[20] For critics, the agreement reflected Chancellor Merkel's economic opportunism and a lack of willingness to consult with the incoming U.S. President Joe Biden's administration.[21] In the spring of 2021, the agreement's ratification was put on ice however, due to EU-China frictions over Chinese human rights violations in the Xinjiang region.

In its December 2021 coalition agreement, the government under Chancellor Olaf Scholz recognized that the agreement could not be finalized "for a number of reasons."[22] At the same time, Berlin has also asserted its intention to intensify efforts for diversification to reduce strong economic dependencies on China, pointing out that Russia's war on Ukraine proved the need for such a move.[23] Nevertheless, Chancellor Scholz's visit to Beijing in November 2022, just days after the conclusion of the 20th Chinese Communist Party Congress, and in the company of a business delegation (though smaller than under previous Chancellor Angela Merkel), cast

---

[17] On the political ties to the trade team in the European Commission, see von der Burchard (2022).
[18] Federal Government/Foreign Ministry, "Policy Guidelines for the Indo-Pacific," 47.
[19] Personal conversations with trade-related officials.
[20] Hilpert (2021).
[21] See for example, Le Corre (2021).
[22] Federal Government (2022).
[23] See for example, Welle (2022).

doubts in the minds of many observer's on his resolve to approach China in a different and more critical way.

In the human rights area, Berlin pursues a two-pronged approach in the Indo-Pacific region[24]: It approaches countries that do not adequately protect political and civil rights with open and critical exchange at the bilateral or multilateral level (e.g., EU or UN) on the one hand, and it supports and promotes civil society on the other. In particular, Germany's financial support for vulnerable societal groups in the Indo-Pacific region has increased recently, with 2022 seeing a doubling of funding compared to the previous year, providing 1.8 million Euro.[25] Given their country's Holocaust history, German policymakers generally feel a special responsibility to defend democracy and human rights.[26]

Chancellor Merkel's human rights policy vis-à-vis China has received mixed reviews, but overall, she was arguably more outspoken about human rights abuses than other European leaders, including French President Emmanuel Macron.[27] During her Chancellorship, she hosted the Dalai Lama in Berlin and successfully pushed Beijing to allow the widow of Nobel peace prize winner Liu Xiaobo to leave China. The Federal Republic also promotes a common European approach to human rights. During Germany's Council presidency, the EU adopted a new human rights sanctions regime in 2020, which was subsequently used to sanction Chinese actors responsible for abuses in Xinjiang. Berlin furthermore passed a law in the summer of 2021, which requires German companies to ensure human rights compliance along their supply chains.[28] These moves show that Berlin is more willing to reconsider the previous compartmentalization of human rights policy and economic engagement, especially vis-à-vis China. The three-party coalition government under Chancellor Scholz has also emphasized its intention to pursue a "values-based" foreign policy that focuses on human rights.[29] In his November 2022 visit to Beijing, Scholz indeed clearly addressed the human rights situation in China, emphasizing that this constituted no interference into a country's internal affairs because of the universal nature of human rights.[30]

Overall, Germany still needs to make efforts to refine its Indo-Pacific approach and its contribution to a rules-based order, tackling a number of difficult questions. One issue is the extent of cooperation with Washington. Europeans in general are uncomfortable with a bipolar frame pitting the U.S. against China, or democracies against autocracies. However, support for liberal internationalism and opposition to Chinese policies inevitably brings Germans and Europeans closer to the United

---

[24] Federal Government/ Foreign Ministry, "Policy Guidelines for the Indo-Pacific," 42.
[25] Federal Government of Germany (2022).
[26] Kinzelbach and Mohan (2016).
[27] Barkin (2021).
[28] Federal Ministry for Economic Cooperation and Development (2022).
[29] SPD and Bündnis 90/Die Grünen und FDP, "Mehr Fortschritt Wagen—Bündnis Für Freiheit, Gerechtigkeit Und Nachhaltigkeit: Koalitionsvertrag 2021–2025," accessed April 28, 2022, https://www.spd.de/fileadmin/Dokumente/Koalitionsvertrag/Koalitionsvertrag_2021-2025.pdf, 113.
[30] See, Deutsche Vertretungen (2022).

States. Berlin also has to reflect further on its "inclusive" approach and how it wants to translate that into practice. With its deployment of the frigate, Germany failed to act as a clear advocate for the rules-based order, rather glossing over critical regional issues by referring to inclusivity. Berlin needs to delineate a more principled stance on questions related to the international order, while also seeking opportunities for dialogue with China. Another issue that Germany must consider is its approach to minilateral cooperation in the Indo-Pacific. So far, Berlin has focused on inclusive, formal institutions like the Association of Southeast Asian Nations (ASEAN) as key pillars that support the regional order. However, cooperation through less formal and ad-hoc minilateralism has proliferated in the Indo-Pacific. While minilaterals may have disadvantages such as the risk of fragmented approaches, they tend to be more effective than inclusive formal institutions in responding to regional needs.

Conclusion

Germany has signaled its resolve to engage the Indo-Pacific region more deeply and comprehensively, but there is still uncertainty in many respects about how to make a constructive contribution to regional stability and the rules-based order and how to balance different policy objectives. The coalition government under Chancellor Scholz has vowed to continue moving forward with the Indo-Pacific policy framework set out by the Merkel government. Against that background, Japan—as a key Indo-Pacific partner for Germany with shared norms and values—should seek to deepen cooperation and share its views and reflections on regional dynamics. During his visit to Tokyo in 2018, then German Foreign Minister Heiko Maas suggested that the two countries can pool their strengths and work with others, aiming to become "rule shapers" that help to design and enhance the international order.[31] Given their status as middle powers, the two countries together can devise new foreign and security policy strategies aimed at contributing to the order that both depend on so fundamentally. They can also help to coopt a wider coalition of states willing to cooperate in this endeavor. The first-ever government consultations that were held between Germany and Japan in March 2023 offered an opportunity to begin discussions on this endeavor.

The Russian invasion in Ukraine is far from over, so assessments about its effect on global as well as German politics can only be preliminary. To some extent, German policymakers may perceive the need to concentrate attention and resources on European affairs. However, the war has also served as a powerful reminder of the importance of defending the global rules-based order to ensure international security and stability of the intricate links between the European and Indo-Pacific security orders. Policymakers in Berlin are not only deeply rattled by Russia's conduct, but also disappointed about China's refusal to clearly condemn the invasion and stand up

---

[31] Federal Foreign Ministry (2022).

for the principle of sovereignty. China's reaction underlines that it would be short-sighted for Berlin to focus only on the European theater and neglect Indo-Pacific affairs. With political resolve, the current crisis can serve as a long-term impetus to solidify cooperation between like-minded countries in Europe and the Indo-Pacific, and shape a common agenda for the rules-based order.

References

Barkin, N. (2021) Rethinking German policy towards China (Chatham House, 2021). https://www.chathamhouse.org/sites/default/files/2021-05/2021-05-26-german-policy-towards-china-barkin.pdf, 7.

Bundeswehr. (2022). Rapid Pacific 2022 (July 22, 2022) Accessed November 25, 2022. https://www.bundeswehr.de/de/organisation/luftwaffe/team-luftwaffe-auf-uebung/rapid-pacific-2022

Daalder, I. H., & Lindsay, J. M. (2018). The committee to save the world order: America's Allies must step up as America steps down. *Foreign Affairs, 97*(6). Accessed 28 April 2022. https://www.foreignaffairs.com/articles/2018-09-30/committee-save-world-order

Deutsche Vertretungen in China. (2022). Statement von Bundeskanzler Olaf Scholz in der Pressekonferenz mit dem chinesischen Ministerpräsidenten Li Keqiang am 4. November 2022 in Peking. November 10, 2022. https://china.diplo.de/cn-de/aktuelles/erklaerungen/-/2562590

Federal Foreign Ministry. (2022). Außenminister Maas Zur Abfahrt Der Fregatte Bayern Nach Asien. Accessed April 28, 2022. https://www.auswaertiges-amt.de/de/newsroom/-/2473486.

Federal Foreign Ministry. (2022). Rede Von Außenminister Heiko Maas Am National Graduate Institute for Policy Studies in Tokyo, Japan. Accessed April 28, 2022, https://www.auswaertiges-amt.de/de/newsroom/maas-japan/2121670.

Federal Government/ Foreign Ministry. (2020). Policy guidelines for the Indo-Pacific.https://www.auswaertiges-amt.de/blob/2380514/f9784f7e3b3fa1bd7c5446d274a4169e/200901-indo-pazifik-leitlinien--1--data.pdf, 2.

Federal Government of Germany. (2022). Progress report on the implementation of the Federal Government policy guidelines for the Indo-Pacific in 2022. (September 6, 2022). Accessed September 15, 2022, https://www.auswaertiges-amt.de/blob/2551720/02b94659532c6af17e40a831bed8fe57/220906-fortschrittsbericht-der-indo-pazifik-leitlinien-data.pdf.

Federal Government. (2022). Mehr Fortschritt wagen: Bündnis für Freiheit, Gerechtigkeit und Nachhaltigkeit. Coalition Agreement between SPD, Bündnis 90/die Grünen, and FDP, November 24, 2022. https://www.bundesregierung.de/resource/blob/974430/1990812/04221173eef9a6720059cc353d759a2b/2021-12-10-koav2021-data.pdf?download=1

Federal Ministry of Defense. (2022). Rede Der Bundesministerin Der Verteidigung Annegret Kramp-Karrenbauer Anlässlich Des Auslaufens Der Fregatte BAYERN Am 2. August 2021. Accessed April 28, 2022. https://www.bmvg.de/resource/blob/5204444/93650740996c0cdf66b1e59f6f119c60/rede-akk-data.pdf.

Federal Ministry for Economic Cooperation and Development. Das Lieferkettengesetz. Accessed April 28, 2022. https://www.bmz.de/de/entwicklungspolitik/lieferkettengesetz

Gerhartz, I. (2022). "Tagesbefehl" (Statement on the Conclusion of Rapid Pacific 2022), October 12, 2022, Accessed November 25, 2022, https://www.bundeswehr.de/resource/blob/5510942/98aa1c176191a66a36357758b489dfaf/download-tagesbefehl-inspl-zu-rapid-pacific-data.pdf

Hilpert, H. G. (2021). New trade agreements in Asia: Liberalisation in times of geopolitical rivalry. SWP Comment C 25 (SWP, 2021).

Ikenberry, G. J. (2022). The plot against American foreign policy: Can the liberal order survive? *Foreign Affairs, 96*(3) (2017). Accessed April 28, 2022. https://www.foreignaffairs.com/articles/united-states/2017-04-17/plot-against-american-foreign-policy

Katrin Kinzelbach and Garima Mohan (2016). German human rights policy in a multipolar world (Global Public Policy Institute, 2016). https://gppi.net/2016/11/21/german-human-rights-policy-in-a-multipolar-world

Kinkartz, S. (2022). Russland Und Die SPD: Scherbenhaufen Der Ostpolitik. [Russia and the SPD: East Policy in Tatters] *DW —Deutsche Welle* (April 21, 2022) Accessed April 28, 2022, https://www.dw.com/de/russland-und-die-spd-scherbenhaufen-der-ostpolitik/a-61204291.

Krauss, E. S., & Maull, H. W. (2020). Germany, Japan and the fate of international order. *Survival, 62*(3). https://doi.org/10.1080/00396338.2020.1763619

Kundnani, H. (2017). What Is the liberal international order? Insights (German Marshall Fund of the United States, 2017), https://www.gmfus.org/news/what-liberal-international-order.

Kundnani, H. & Tsuruoka, M. (2021) Germany's Indo-Pacific frigate may send unclear message. Expert Comment (Chatham House, 2021). https://www.chathamhouse.org/2021/05/germanys-indo-pacific-frigate-may-send-unclear-message.

Le Corre, P.. Europe's Tightrope Diplomacy on China (Carnegie Endowment for International Peace, 2021). https://carnegieendowment.org/2021/03/24/europe-s-tightrope-diplomacy-on-china-pub-84159

Nouwens, V., & Mohan, G. (2021). Europe eyes the Indo-Pacific, but now It's time to act. *War on the Rocks* (June 24, 2021) accessed April 28, 2022, https://warontherocks.com/2021/06/europe-eyes-the-indo-pacific-but-now-its-time-to-act/

von der Burchard, H. (2022). Merkel pushes EU-China investment deal over the finish line despite criticism. *POLITICO* (December 29, 2020). Accessed April 28, 2022, https://www.politico.eu/article/eu-china-investment-deal-angela-merkel-pushes-finish-line-despite-criticism/

Welle, D. (2022). Germany seeks less China reliance after Russia 'mistake' (November 22, 2022) https://www.dw.com/en/germany-seeks-less-china-reliance-after-russia-mistake/a-63848899

Open Access This chapter is licensed under the terms of the Creative Commons Attribution-NonCommercial-NoDerivatives 4.0 International License (http://creativecommons.org/licenses/by-nc-nd/4.0/), which permits any noncommercial use, sharing, distribution and reproduction in any medium or format, as long as you give appropriate credit to the original author(s) and the source, provide a link to the Creative Commons license and indicate if you modified the licensed material. You do not have permission under this license to share adapted material derived from this chapter or parts of it.

The images or other third party material in this chapter are included in the chapter's Creative Commons license, unless indicated otherwise in a credit line to the material. If material is not included in the chapter's Creative Commons license and your intended use is not permitted by statutory regulation or exceeds the permitted use, you will need to obtain permission directly from the copyright holder.

Chapter 6
France's Indo-Pacific Approach: Salvaging the Rules-Based Order and Staying Relevant

Céline Pajon

Abstract As a P5 country and an Indo-Pacific nation, France aims to act as a balancing power that would offer an alternative to the choice between China and the United States, which is increasingly faced by countries around the world, especially in the Indo-Pacific. The "Macron Doctrine" is set to make France consolidate its role as a balancing, united, radiant, influential power, a driving force for European autonomy that preserves the multilateral mechanisms based on international law. The trilateral security pact between Australia, the United Kingdom and the United States (AUKUS) shock of 2021 was a blow for Paris, but France distances itself from upholding a continued U.S. dominance, and defines its strategy as complementary with that of the U.S. Seeing China as a destabilizing factor in the Indo-Pacific (French Defense Strategy 2021) and a systemic rival (National Strategic Review 2022) of liberal international order, France supports a multipolar order that would allow for it to pursue its own approach, while also reducing China's influence in the region.

Upholding the rules-based order[1] is a significant objective of the French Indo-Pacific (IP) strategy that was unveiled in 2018.[2] France was the first European country to adopt such a strategy. The vast region is indeed identified as a key arena where international norms are being challenged, and the future world order, shaped by the US-China rivalry, is at play. France is also a resident power in the IP, with overseas territories in the Indian and Pacific oceans, 1.5 million citizens, and a large exclusive economic zone (EEZ).[3] The preservation of the rules-based order in the IP thus

---
[1] French official documents (xxxx).
[2] Emmanuel Macron (2018).
[3] France is a resident power in the region (xxxx).

C. Pajon (✉)
Head of Japan Research, Center for Asian Studies, French Institute of International Relations, Paris, France

© The International House of Japan, Inc. 2024
Y. Hosoya and H. Kundnani (eds.), *The Transformation of the Liberal International Order*, SpringerBriefs in International Relations,
https://doi.org/10.1007/978-981-99-4729-4_6

participates in shaping a favorable geostrategic order and relates to France's national interests in the region, as well as to Paris' universalist ambition.

Stating, along with Hans Kundnani, that the rules-based order includes three pillars: the security, the economic, and the human rights orders, we argue that France, due to its sovereign interests in the area, is primarily focusing on the security dimension of the rules-based order and expects to promote the economic and human rights dimensions more efficiently through the EU Indo-Pacific strategy.[4] France was indeed the leading engine behind the adoption of such strategy. This paper aims at analyzing the significance of the rules-based order for France's IP strategy and discusses its recent developments and challenges.

China's Challenge to the Rules-Based Order and Macron's Diplomacy: Two Important Drivers for the French Indo-Pacific Strategy

In the past decade, several developments in the IP region have been closely monitored and have served as catalysts to prompt the definition of a French strategic vision. In particular, the advance of China in the South China Sea and the risks it posed to the freedom of navigation and the peaceful resolution of disputes is one important element, as well as the development of the Belt and Road Initiative (BRI) (2013) that spreads all the way to the Indian ocean and Europe.[5] The opening of a large Chinese base in Djibouti in 2017 was a wake-up call, and the various implications of China's BRI convinced the Foreign Affairs and the Ministry of Economy of the necessity to better define the national interest and strategy vis à vis China, including in the Indo-Pacific.[6] The 2017 Strategic Review of Defense and National Security clearly acknowledged the risks of China's rise, in terms of strategic ambition ("becoming the dominant power in Asia" and "surpass[ing] the American power"); military buildup ("the Chinese army [...] is now more than four times higher than that of France") and challenge to the rules-based order (in particular in the South China Sea, "where Beijing invokes "historical rights" and employs methods such as the reclamation of certain islets").[7] The French Defense Strategy in 2021 describes the expansion of China as a destabilizing factor in the Indo-Pacific, shifting the balance of power, challenging democratic values and triggering strong security concerns.[8] The National Strategic Review of November 2022 clarifies the vision of China as a systemic rival—"[...] the Chinese regime believes that Western leadership in the international order has weakened and that it can weaken it further by using its new influence. [...] such questioning irrigates fields which are political (propaganda on the decline

---

[4] Hans Kundnani (2017).
[5] Hugo Meijer (2021).
[6] Alice Ekman (2018).
[7] Strategic Review of Defense (2017).
[8] China's close relation (2019).

of the West), economic and technological (predation, trade war), military (growth of the nuclear arsenal, modernization of the PLA, areas of support abroad), and diplomatic"—and notes with concern the growing strategic convergence between Beijing and Moscow.[9] France, a P5 country and an Indo-Pacific nation, is legitimate to act as sovereign power and also a responsible stakeholder in the area.

Upon his arrival in 2017, President Macron indeed made clear that he wanted to restore France's global influence by upholding its values and principles and for Paris to be a central player for global governance and multilateralism.[10] This approach is reaffirmed by Macron in the latest Strategic Review: "By 2030, I want France to have consolidated its role as a balancing, united, radiant, influential power, a driving force for European autonomy and one that assumes its responsibilities by contributing, as a reliable and supportive partner, to the preservation of multilateral mechanisms based on international law."[11] The "Macron Doctrine" is based on a sense of deep crisis of the world order: "We see that we have a crisis with the multilateral framework of 1945: a crisis in terms of its effectiveness, but, and it is even more serious in my opinion, a crisis in terms of the universality of the values upheld by its structures."[12]

Russia and China are clearly identified as powers that play down human rights and liberal values and principles. Macron has repeatedly underlined, especially during its visits to France's territories in the region, the risks of a Chinese hegemony and the need for Paris to develop its own approach in the Indo-Pacific and act as a credible power there.[13]

In the Indo-Pacific, France is thus primarily committed to support the security dimension of the rules-based order—especially maritime security. France is also, however, committed to environmental security as a key focus. Only a modest mention of the human rights appears in the 2022 IP Strategy referring to the respect of these rights in implementing France's public development assistance projects.[14] The "values" dimension of the French IP approach should be understood broadly, as the promotion of international law and a democratic process emphasized at the inter-state level (in the form of a new multilateralism), rather than at domestic level (allowing an inclusive approach aiming at federating a maximum of like-minded partners). The economic dimension of the rules-based order is to be carried out primarily at the European level, as France has only limited means to promote connectivity, and as the EU has the exclusive competence on trade.[15]

---

[9] The National Strategic (2022).

[10] Discours du Président (2017).

[11] The National Strategic (2022).

[12] Emmanuel Macron (2020).

[13] In this region of the globe (2018).

[14] In a global (2022).

[15] The French Development Agency (AFD) (xxx).

Advancing the Three Pillars of the Rules-Based Order, with a Focus on Security

At the core of France's principle-based approach in the IP are the freedom of maritime and aerial circulation and the respect of international law, especially at sea.[16] Freedom of Navigation (FON) stands out as one of the key concerns for France: any disruption of the vital maritime routes would indeed be dramatic for European economic and trade security.

Accordingly, France supports the strict application of the United Nations Convention for the Law of the Sea (UNCLOS), contributes to actions against crime at sea, and is keen on actively demonstrating its commitment to the FON. In 2016, at the Shangri-La Dialogue, then Minister of Defense Jean-Yves Le Drian emphasized the need to discourage unilateral *coups de force* in the China seas, for fear that such actions might expand in other areas like the Mediterranean Sea.[17] Thus, while not taking sides on sovereignty matters, Paris has consistently sent its ships to the South and East China Seas in recent years, through the passing of the Jeanne d'Arc mission or the surveillance frigates based in New Caledonia. In June 2019, the aircraft carrier *Charles de Gaulle* was dispatched to Singapore. The French Minister of the Armed Forces, Florence Parly, then promised that French vessels would sail at least twice a year in the South China Sea and will continue upholding international law in a "steady, non-confrontational but obstinate way."[18] In the beginning of 2021, a French nuclear-powered submarine (SSN) patrolled the area, demonstrating the capacity to deploy far away, in coordination with strategic partners, "to affirm that international law is the only rule that is valid."[19]

From the same perspective, France aims to develop maritime surveillance capabilities in the region, as Maritime Domain Awareness (MDA) is a requirement for better managing one's own sovereign territory and EEZ but also to ensure the safety of international waters, SLOCs, and FON. In this way, maritime surveillance (contributing to enhance environmental security) is an enabling approach to act in the region, with partners, for the common goods, but also to uphold norms and strengthen territorial control.[20]

Paris has strongly pushed the European Union to adopt its own Indo-Pacific approach, announced on September 16, 2021.[21] France is eager to coordinate at the EU level in the Indo-Pacific because an EU approach works both in synergy with France (particularly on maritime security)[22] and also as a complement to the French

---

[16] France's Indo-Pacific (2022).

[17] Jean-Yves Le Drian (2016).

[18] Discours de Florence (2019).

[19] A series of tweet (2021).

[20] Thibault Fournol (2019).

[21] Joint Communication (2021).

[22] The EU ministerial (2022).

strategy. Indeed, the EU has significant capacities to support sustainable development, infrastructures and capacity building through its 2018 EU-Asia Connectivity Strategy, and its Global Gateway Initiative announced in December 2021.[23] The EU, as a trade superpower, has also a greater leverage in this domain (especially by concluding Economic Partnership Agreements) and Brussels is also looking to become a strategic player on critical technologies. The EU's Indo-Pacific strategy has a strong focus on building resilient value chains, especially in semiconductors, including by possibly setting up a deal with Taiwan. In addition, standards setting in trade, digital domains and emerging technologies, "in line with democratic principles," is one of the prior objectives of the EU's IP approach. The EU has also been a consistent defender of human rights, not least of all with the set of sanctions adopted in March 2021 vis-a-vis China to protest the large-scale arbitrary detentions of Uyghurs in Xinjiang.[24] The Indo-Pacific strategy also mentions that "the EU will continue to protect its essential interests and promote its values while pushing back where fundamental disagreements exist with China, such as on human rights."[25]

Working with the EU level will allow France to promote a more holistic strategy in the region and facilitate France's vision to act as a balancing and mediating power, providing an alternative to the Sino-US competition.

A "Balancing Power"? Strategic Autonomy and the Aims to Foster a Stable Rules-Based Order

France (and the EU) is advocating a strategic autonomy on the international scene, including in the Indo-Pacific. Paris has indeed been uncomfortable with a Washington IP policy that has been Sino-centric, military-based, and confrontational. Instead, it is promoting an independent and inclusive IP strategy, reflecting a slightly different vision of what should be a stable, rules-based order. Rather than upholding continued U.S. dominance, France supports a multipolar order that would allow for it to pursue its own approach, while also reducing China's influence in the region.

In addition, Paris considers that the US-China rivalry (in addition to China's own assertive moves) is a disruptive factor,[26] and aims to mitigate the negative side-effect of the growing polarization by fostering a multipolar and multilateral region governed by the rule of law: "Beyond any logic of blocks, we therefore intend to champion a third path in the Indo-Pacific, for responding to today's upheavals with all well-intentioned powers."[27] President Macron emphasizes that France should be a

---

[23] Team Europe (2021).
[24] EU imposes (2021).
[25] The EU strategy (xxxx).
[26] Chinese-American (2022).
[27] Foreword by Jean-Yves Le Drian (2021).

"balancing power"[28] (*puissance d'équilibre(s)*), not aligned, but acting independently and offering an alternative out of the bipolar confrontation.

This explains why France, while maintaining close and dynamic strategic partnerships with the four members of the Quad (Quadrilateral Security Dialogue), has so far refused to be politically associated with the grouping. Not only the Quad is perceived by some as an anti-China coalition, but Paris prefers to keep its options open and promote its own initiatives. France's IP strategy is thus based on a number of close partnerships, founded upon common values and similar interests, and strives to build up a network in order to mutualize capacity and have a greater impact. Partners includes India, Japan, the U.S. and Australia (to a lesser extent after AUKUS), but also Indonesia and Singapore, among others. Southeast Asia being the main ground for the Great Game between China and the U.S., ensuring its resilience to resist the Chinese expansion and mitigate the Sino-U.S. competition is key. In addition, Paris promotes an "effective multilateralism, based on the rule of law and the rejection of coercion" to "encourage cooperative approaches, rather than operating via blocks."[29] France is indeed an active member of a number of regional organizations in the Indo-Pacific.[30] Minilateral and ad hoc groupings are also considered useful as an "effective form of multilateralism" and should be privileged to discuss and adopt a shared understanding and common principles to tackle issues, from climate change to governance of the commons (oceans, internet).

The AUKUS Shock and the Sustainability of France's Approach

This middle way approach of France in the Indo-Pacific is not without challenges. The announcement of the the trilateral security pact between Australia, the United Kingdom and the United States (AUKUS) in September 2021 was a shock. Paris was never consulted, nor notified in advance, despite the historic importance of the deal and the huge implications for France's interests, not least the brutal termination of the submarine contract with Canberra. AUKUS provoked a crisis of confidence in France's relations with its three key partners and also shed light on the divergences regarding the best way to salvage the rules-based order and address the China challenge.[31] It called into question France's strategic positioning in the Indo-Pacific, and the risk of being side-lined as the Sino-U.S. rivalry was deepening, pushing for alignment with the U.S. For Paris, it only urged the Europeans to accelerate the path towards better defining and protecting their interests.[32]

---

[28] Discours du Président (2019).

[29] France's Indo-Pacific (2022).

[30] France is part of the Indian (xxxx).

[31] The United States (xxxx).

[32] France hopes to salvage (2021).

Actually, the demonstrations of European support and solidarity with France in the wake of the AUKUS shock were fewer than expected, and various criticisms were voiced—more or less openly—by politicians in EU member countries disapproving of France's "Europeanisation" of the AUKUS crisis.[33] Indeed, a number of Eastern European countries are very much dependent on the U.S. for their security. These countries support a European engagement in the Indo-Pacific as a quid pro quo for a lasting American security commitment in Europe, and want to avoid unnecessary tensions with their ally.

These reactions show the reluctance of European partners to align with an IP approach that favors strategic autonomy at the expense of the relationship with Washington. Paris will have to make its position explicit: strategic autonomy is often interpreted as the sign of a wavering commitment to the IP, or of an equidistant positioning between the U.S. and China—which it is not. France must be clear that it shares Washington's core values but wishes to keep some room to maneuver vis à vis certain U.S. choices driven by interests Paris might not share.

Working on a close coordination and a complementarity with the U.S. will thus be key in implementing a French and EU policy in the region. Upholding the rule of law at sea is a key issue in the Indo-Pacific, but not all the issues—including but not limited to the law of the sea, sustainable development, climate security, fisheries management, piracy—relate to hard security. Europeans have a very limited military capacity to commit to the IP, but have extensive expertise and experience in these subjects. France and the EU can thus demonstrate their added value by working as a complement to the United States' more militaristic approach in the IP.

Conclusion

France's Indo-Pacific strategy aims to build up a stable region governed by the rule of law, to protect itself against threats (including from China) and to mitigate the risks of great powers competition in a key area. It reflects important concerns about its core national interests and identity, pertaining to sovereignty, but also to its values and diplomatic status. From this perspective, the Indo-Pacific is both an area to exercise this strategic autonomy and enables a narrative to support France's ambition to act as a European power with global reach, actively supporting a rules-based order, and act as a "balancing power."

Considering this constructivist dimension of France's engagement in the Indo-Pacific somewhat explains the gap between the political rhetoric of an Indo-Pacific "priority" for France and the reality of the resources to engage in this area.[34] Some in Paris have questioned the relevance of an IP strategy.[35] Actually, this approach also

---

[33] Pacte Aukus (2021).
[34] The Indo-Pacific region (xxxx)
[35] Jean-Dominique Merchet (2018).

serves the broader French diplomatic agenda under Macron: to ensure France's relevance and status in the coming world order. The pandemics, or the war in Ukraine have not changed the French calculus but rather exemplified the importance of the developments in the Indo-Pacific for France's interests and the interconnection between the Asian and European theatres. The growing tensions in the Taiwan Strait, however, urge France to explain should an open conflict break out, which would have global destabilizing consequences.

References

A series of tweet by Florence Parly on February 8, 2021 and Xavier Vavasseur, "A French Navy SSN Patrolled the South China Sea," *Naval News* (9 February 2021).
Alice Ekman [Eds.], "La France face aux Nouvelles Routes de la Soie chinoise," *Etude de l'Ifri*, October 2018. Available at: www.ifri.org; "Les nouvelles routes de la soie,"*Trésoréco*, n°229, Direction générale du Trésor, Ministry of the Economy and Finance (October 2018). https://www.tresor.economie.gouv.fr/Articles/1f64b246-7e41-4284-8de5-b079aecb5b7e/files/7fb43132-5583-4e63-917a-8e2a505c909a.
Between 2021 and 2027, Team Europe, meaning the EU institutions and EU Member States jointly, will mobilize up to 300 billion euros of investments for this initiative: See the webpage of the European Commission dedicated to the Global Gateway: https://ec.europa.eu/info/strategy/priorities-2019-2024/stronger-europe-world/global-gateway_en.
China's close relation with Russia in challenging democratic values, its enduring support to North Korea, its strategic partnership with Pakistan, the ongoing borders issues with India as well as the territorial disputes in the East and South China seas generate deep-seated concerns regarding the implications of China's actions." France's Defense Strategy in the Indo-Pacific (2019) p. 8.
Chinese-American strategic competition and the behaviour of certain regional actors, giving priority to bilateral arrangements and power relations in order to favour their own national interests, contribute to the breakdown of the international order, while global challenges are requiring greater cooperation from States. The risks of uncontrolled escalation are great in this region, which lacks crisis regulation mechanisms. In line with the principles and values demonstrated in its international commitment, France works for a multilateral international order that is based on the rule of law. 2022 Strategy, p. 10.
Discours de Florence Parly, ministre des Armées, Allocution au Shangri-La Dialogue (1st June 2019). https://www.defense.gouv.fr/salle-de-presse/discours/discours-de-florence-parly/discours-de-florence-parly-ministre-des-armees_allocution-au-shangri-la-dialogue.
Discours du Président de la République à la conférence des Ambassadeurs, Paris (29 August 2017) https://www.elysee.fr/emmanuel-macron/2017/08/29/discours-du-president-de-la-republique-a-l-ouverture-de-la-conference-des-ambassadeurs.
Discours du Président de la République à la conférence des Ambassadeurs, Paris (August 27, 2019) https://www.elysee.fr/front/pdf/elysee-module-14146-fr.pdf.
Emmanuel Macron, "Speech at Garden Island Naval Base," Sydney (May 2, 2018). https://www.elysee.fr/emmanuel-macron/2018/05/03/discours-a-garden-island-base-navale-de-sydney. The most updated and comprehensive document has been published in February 2022: "France's Indo-Pacific Strategy 2022," Ministry for Europe and Foreign Affairs: https://www.diplomatie.gouv.fr/IMG/pdf/en_dcp_a4_indopacifique_022022_v1-4_web_cle878143.pdf.
Emmanuel Macron, Gilles Gressani, Mathéo Malik, Ramona Bloj, "The Macron Doctrine," GEG (November 2020) https://geopolitique.eu/en/2020/11/16/the-macron-doctrine/.

EU imposes further sanctions over serious violations of human rights around the world, Council of the European Union (March22, 2021) https://www.consilium.europa.eu/en/press/press-releases/2021/03/22/eu-imposes-further-sanctions-over-serious-violations-of-human-rights-around-the-world/.

Foreword by Jean-Yves Le Drian, in *France's Partnerships in the Indo-Pacific,* Ministry of Europe and Foreign Affairs (April 2021a) https://www.diplomatie.gouv.fr/en/photos-publications-and-graphics/publications/article/france-s-partnerships-in-the-indo-pacific-apr-2021a.

France's Indo-Pacific Strategy 2022, p. 3.

France is part of the Indian Ocean Commission, the Indian Ocean Naval Symposium (IONS), the West Pacific Naval Symposium (WPNS), the Indian Ocean Rim Association, the South Pacific Defence Ministers' Meeting (SPDMM), the Heads of Asian Coast Guard Agencies Meeting, a Dialogue Partner of the Pacific Islands Forum and a Development Partner of ASEAN. Paris is applying for an observer status to the ASEAN Defense Ministers Meeting+ (ADMM+).

France hopes to salvage EU autonomy from submarine deal wreckage, *The Financial Times* (September 21, 2021b) https://www.ft.com/content/049638c2-ccf9-4fea-a860-203a7e26c566.

France's Indo-Pacific Strategy 2022, p. 3.

French official documents and decision-makers are generally using the term of "rules-based order" rather than "liberal international order," in order to prevent any misunderstanding on the meaning of "liberal" in this context and also avoid antagonizing non-democratic countries.

France is a resident power in the region, maintaining territories both in the Indian Ocean (Islands of Mayotte and La Réunion, the Scattered Islands and the French Southern and Antarctic Territories) and the Pacific (New Caledonia, Wallis and Futuna, French Polynesia and Clipperton Island), with 1.5 million citizens living there and in other countries in the region (approximately 200,000 people), and more than 90% of its large EEZ (9 million km^2) located in the two oceans. France maintains a military presence of 8,000 personnel to take care of this vast area.

Hans Kundnani, "What is the Liberal International Order?" *Insights*, GMFUS (3 May 2017) https://www.gmfus.org/news/what-liberal-international-order#_ftn13.

Hugo Meijer, "Pulled East. The rise of China, Europe and French security policy in the Asia-Pacific," *Journal of Strategic Studies* (2021).

In this region of the globe, China is building its hegemony step by step. […] We should work with China […] to intensify exchanges and seize all the opportunities, but if we don't organize ourselves, it will soon be a hegemony that will reduce our freedoms, our opportunities and that we will have to endure." (Author's Translation—Check the original delivery) Discours du Président de la République Emmanuel Macron sur la Nouvelle-Calédonie à Nouméa (5 May 2018) https://www.elysee.fr/front/pdf/elysee-module-2070-fr.pdf. Referring to China without naming it, in Papeete: "But I tell you very clearly, in the times that are opening up, woe to the little ones, woe to the isolated, woe to those who will have to endure influence and incursions of hegemons that will come to seek their fish, their technologies, their economic resources. (Author's Translation—Check the original delivery.) Discours du Président de la République à Papeete, Tahiti (28 July 2021) https://www.elysee.fr/front/pdf/elysee-module-18162-fr.pdf.

In a global context where the universal nature of human rights is being called into question, France supports protecting these values, particularly in the Indo-Pacific, as part of its commitment to the rule of law. France's Indo-Pacific Strategy 2022, p. 14.

Jean-Yves Le Drian, Minister of Defense, France—Statement for the fourth plenary session: The challenges of conflict resolution, 15th Asia Security Summit, The IISS Shangri-La Dialogue, Singapore (5 June 2016). Retrieved from https://www.iiss.org/events/shangri-la-dialogue/shangri-la-dialogue-2016.

Jean-Dominique Merchet, "L''axe indopacifique' est-il un piège pour la France ?" *Blog Secret Défense* (November 2, 2018).

Joint Communication to the European Parliament and the Council, The EU strategy for cooperation in the Indo-Pacific (September 16, 2021) https://eeas.europa.eu/sites/default/files/jointcommunication_2021_24_1_en.pdf.

Pacte Aukus : il est temps que l'UE se positionne, *Courrier International* (September 27, 2021), or Ido Vock, Why EU support for France over Aukus has been muted, *The New Stateman* (September 22, 2021).

The National Strategic Review (November 2022a) http://www.sgdsn.gouv.fr/communiques_presse/revue-nationale-strategique-2022a/

The National Strategic Review (November 2022b) op. cit.

The French Development Agency (AFD) is primarily focusing on environmental projects in the region and therefore cannot promote connectivity in other ways or through other projects.

The EU ministerial Forum on the Indo-Pacific held in Paris on February 22, 2022, announced that a EU Coordinated Maritime Presence will be soon set up for the first time in the Indo-Pacific, precisely in the Northwestern Indian Ocean. Between 2021 and 2027, Team Europe, meaning the EU institutions and EU Member States jointly, will mobilize up to 300 billion euros of investments for this initiative: See the webpage of the European Commission dedicated to the Global Gateway: https://ec.europa.eu/info/strategy/priorities-2019-2024/stronger-europe-world/global-gateway_en.

The EU strategy for cooperation in the Indo-Pacific, p. 4.

The United States is an ally and a major Indo-Pacific player with which France wishes to maintain close cooperation. Our approaches may diverge, as shown by the AUKUS affair, but we are seeking synergy between our Indo-Pacific strategies. The aim is to contribute to our shared goal of an open, stable region, based on the rule of law," on the website of the Ministry of Europe and Foreign Affairs: https://www.diplomatie.gouv.fr/en/country-files/asia-and-oceania/the-indo-pacific-region-a-priority-for-france/article/indo-pacific-questions-and-answers-on-france-s-regional-strategy.

The Indo-Pacific region: a priority for France. Ministry of European and Foreign Affairs, https://www.diplomatie.gouv.fr/en/country-files/asia-and-oceania/the-indo-pacific-region-a-priority-for-france/.

Thibault Fournol, "La sécurité environnementale : émergence d'une stratégie de défense française en Indo-Pacifique," *Mémoire de Master*, Sciences Po Paris (2019).

2017 Strategic Review of Defense and National Security—Paris (October 2017). https://www.google.com/url?sa=t&rct=j&q=&esrc=s&source=web&cd=&ved=2ahUKEwj3toWyocn3AhVD5IUKHVbCBm0QFnoECBAQAQ&url=https%3A%2F%2Ffranceintheus.org%2FIMG%2Fpdf%2Fdefense_and_national_security_strategic_review_2017.pdf&usg=AOvVaw3GHS_bQpgoKUYtuiaqtXmS. Translation by the author (p. 42–43).

Open Access This chapter is licensed under the terms of the Creative Commons Attribution-NonCommercial-NoDerivatives 4.0 International License (http://creativecommons.org/licenses/by-nc-nd/4.0/), which permits any noncommercial use, sharing, distribution and reproduction in any medium or format, as long as you give appropriate credit to the original author(s) and the source, provide a link to the Creative Commons license and indicate if you modified the licensed material. You do not have permission under this license to share adapted material derived from this chapter or parts of it.

The images or other third party material in this chapter are included in the chapter's Creative Commons license, unless indicated otherwise in a credit line to the material. If material is not included in the chapter's Creative Commons license and your intended use is not permitted by statutory regulation or exceeds the permitted use, you will need to obtain permission directly from the copyright holder.

Chapter 7
India, the Quad, and the Liberal International Order

Dhruva Jaishankar

Abstract After the Covid-19 pandemic and Russia's invasion of Ukraine, China stands out as the predominant challenger to India's international interests and the international order. Despite its tradition of a post-colonial, developing democracy that was non-aligned during the Cold War, India upholds the rules-based international order together with the U.S., Europe and Japan. Quad is one of the most important new arrangements to upheld a rules-based international order in the Indo-Pacific. At the same time, India has sought to retain a leadership role in the Global South, given concerns about China's growing influence. Besides defending the rules-based international order, India has also been a staunch defender of national sovereignty, and believes that the open trading system has not always offered a level playing field. India will simultaneously seek cooperation with the Quad, the middle-powers outside the Quad and the Global South, so that critical technology and best practices necessary for India's transformation and increased leverage are secured.

As a post-colonial, developing democracy that was non-aligned during the Cold War, India has traditionally been ambivalent when it comes to the common American, European, or Japanese conceptions of the liberal international order. On the one hand, India has frequently worked to uphold a rules-based international order and recognizes the material and normative benefits of international security and stability, open and fair economic engagement, and the governance of the global commons.[1] At the same time, India has been a staunch defender of national sovereignty.[2] It has also argued that an open trading system has not always offered a level playing field.[3] Furthermore, India's leadership perceives the current governing institutions of the

---

[1] Modi (2018).

[2] Puri (2016).

[3] Jaishankar (2020a).

D. Jaishankar (✉)
Observer Research Foundation America, Washington, DC, USA

© The International House of Japan, Inc. 2024
Y. Hosoya and H. Kundnani (eds.), *The Transformation of the Liberal International Order*, SpringerBriefs in International Relations,
https://doi.org/10.1007/978-981-99-4729-4_7

international order as fundamentally unequal and unrepresentative.[4] These considerations have sometimes put it at odds with the political, economic, and international relations conceptions of "liberalism" often associated with the liberal international order. Not surprisingly, Indian officials and commentators eschew the nostalgia for the liberal international order that often characterizes discourse in the United States, Europe, and Japan.

In recent years, three major developments—the rise of China, the COVID-19 pandemic, and the Russian invasion of Ukraine—have significantly shaped India's approach to the international system. On some matters, India has felt compelled to take further steps to uphold a rules-based international order, as on the law of the sea, climate mitigation and adaptation, emerging technologies, connectivity infrastructure, and trade agreements with trusted partners.[5] In a few cases, as on climate and connectivity, this has even required India to assume a greater leadership role. At the same time, India has also sought to deepen its partnership with the United States, the European Union (and its member states), Japan, the United Kingdom, Australia, and other U.S. allies in order to respond to emerging challenges. The Quadrilateral Security Dialogue (Quad)—involving Australia, India, Japan, and the United States—represents the most prominent expression of these twin objectives in the Indo-Pacific.[6] India has also sought to retain a leadership role in the Global South, given concerns about China's growing influence. This has occasionally put India at odds with the United States and its allies.[7]

For the foreseeable future, India is likely to perceive China as the predominant challenger to its own international interests and the international order. This will contribute to the deepening of the Quad partnership as a vehicle for upholding the international order in the Indo-Pacific. At the same time, given concerns about U.S. staying power, India has invested in a proliferation of issue-specific "middle-power" coalitions, also involving France, Japan, Australia, and Indonesia, among others.[8] A further series of parallel steps involves a deepening of economic and technical partnerships with the United States and its allies—including both the European Union and Japan—in an effort to internally balance and thus strengthen Indian capabilities. These countries still constitute a large proportion of the global economy and—outside China and Russia—would be the likely sources of critical technology and best practices necessary for India's transformation.

Despite these simultaneous efforts by India to partner with the United States, Japan, Australia, the European Union and its member states such as France, in

---

[4] Akbaruddin (2021).

[5] Jha (2021), Rehman (2017), "Official Spokesperson's Response to a Query on Participation of India in OBOR/BRI Forum," Ministry of External Affairs, Government of India (May 13, 2017), Arakkal (2021); "Joint Statement from Founding Members of the Global Partnership on Artificial Intelligence," U.S. Department of State (June 15, 2020).

[6] Jaishankar and Madan (2021, 2022).

[7] Thakkar (2021).

[8] Madan (2020a).

support of a more stable international order, there will continue to be complications and limitations. India's traditional concerns about the inequities and nature of the liberal international order will almost certainly become a recurring theme in bilateral and multilateral negotiations. A second factor will involve competing calculations reflecting India's role in the Global South. Both dynamics will continue to create divergences in perceptions and policies with even close partners, despite many aspects of bilateral and multilateral cooperation with the established democracies that continue to uphold a rules-based international order.

India's Ambivalence About the Liberal International Order

Despite its close association with nonalignment during the Cold War, India in fact had a more complex and multifaceted relationship with the U.S.-led liberal international order since independence. India was a founding member of the United Nations, a participant in the Bretton Woods conference, and among the initial signatories of the General Agreement on Tariffs and Trade (GATT), the precursor to the World Trade Organization.[9] It received significant aid from the United States and allies between 1947 and the 1960s, including technical assistance, agricultural technology, and military support.[10] It also took part in UN military and peacekeeping missions, whether in Korea or in Congo.[11] This changed after 1971, and was reflected during the latter half of the Cold War, when India—concerned about a U.S.-China-Pakistan partnership—entered into a treaty with the Soviet Union.[12]

The 1990s were a period of transition, defined by India's gradual economic opening after 1991 and questions about its nuclear status. Following its 1998 nuclear tests, however, India embarked upon active diplomatic outreach efforts with the United States, Japan, and Australia, as well as France and other European powers.[13] By 2008, this resulted in the effective mainstreaming of India's nuclear weapon program, ensuring that it was on a stronger footing to engage with the international community on defense and sensitive technologies. Nonetheless, the period between 2008 and 2014 witnessed India partnering with China and Russia in a bid to negotiate a stronger position for itself in the international order, resulting in such coalitions as BRICS, the Asian Infrastructure Investment Bank (AIIB), and the BASIC coalition on climate change.

Despite efforts to engage Beijing, India's relations with China grew more competitive after about 2012. Indian and Chinese forces faced off on their disputed border in 2013, 2014, 2017, and 2020–22, with the latter crisis resulting in the first military casualties on both sides in over four decades. Greater Chinese influence in South Asia

---

[9] Rajadhyaksha (2019).
[10] Madan (2020b), Engerman (2018).
[11] Bhagavan (2019), Raghavan (2016).
[12] Singh (2019).
[13] Talbott (2004).

and the Indian Ocean region, often under the umbrella of the Belt and Road Initiative, exacerbated regional tensions. The permanent presence of China in the Indian Ocean region necessitated recasting the wider region as a single strategic continuum: the Indo-Pacific. Chinese intransigence at multilateral institutions and on economic and trade concerns contributed even further to deteriorating relations with India. These tensions were exacerbated by two further shocks: the COVID-19 pandemic in 2020 and the resulting disruption in supply chains, as well as the Russia-Ukraine war of 2022 and the very direct impact for India's energy and food security.

Collectively, these developments have accelerated several trends that had begun gradually after 2000. Most notable has been India's growing relationship with the United States and its allies. Relations with Japan steadily grew but accelerated during Shinzo Abe's period as prime minister.[14] India's relations with Australia were traditionally marked by greater suspicion but major breakthroughs followed after 2019.[15] At the same time, India's partnership with France—a country that opposed sanctions against India after its 1998 nuclear tests—assumed a strategic dimension, encompassing defense, civil nuclear, and maritime security cooperation. After difficulties, including over bilateral issues involving Italy and Denmark, India-EU relations also broadened, resulting eventually in the establishment of a Trade and Technology Council.[16] The consequence of all this has been a network of interstitial military and economic arrangements that have resulted in much more cooperative and trusted partnerships between India, on the one hand, and the developed democracies allied to the United States.

The Quad: Necessary but Insufficient

The Quad involving Australia, India, Japan, and the United States, has emerged as one—perhaps the most important—new arrangement to uphold a rules-based international order in the Indo-Pacific. Its antecedents stem from the 2004 Indian Ocean tsunami, after which the four navies quickly coordinated relief efforts. In 2007, officials from the four countries met in Manila and the four navies—along with Singapore—conducted a multilateral naval exercise. Quadrilateral cooperation stopped in 2008 following an Australian decision, but there was in any case little enthusiasm in all four capitals for continuing the partnership given equities with China.[17] In 2017, the Quad was revived, was gradually upgraded to the ministerial level, and in 2021 to the leadership level.

Since 2021, the Quad has developed into a series of issue-specific working groups, rather than continue as either a talk shop or an overly bureaucratized international

---

[14] Basrur and Kutty (2018).

[15] Jaishankar (2020b).

[16] "EU-India: Joint Press Release on Launching the Trade and Technology Council," European Commission (April 25, 2022).

[17] Flitton (2020).

organization. Quadrilateral defense cooperation continues with the Malabar naval exercise, but the Quad is now working towards specific outcomes on maritime domain awareness, green transportation, supply chains, COVID-19 vaccines, scientific education and research, cybersecurity, 5G telecommunications, infrastructure, humanitarian assistance, and space-based earth observation.[18] All these efforts are driven by a desire to demonstrate meaningful impact in providing global public goods, making the Quad appear less exclusive and threatening to partners in the Indo-Pacific, and shoring up the regional order.

Despite the considerable progress made and the importance given to the Quad by the four countries' leaders, it is not a panacea for the challenges facing the international order in the Indo-Pacific. Many of those challenges—whether concerning territorial disputes, arms control, unfair trade practices, and interference—will have to be addressed either through bilateral engagement with China or through other means. The question of Taiwan—involving the United States as well as Japan—is perhaps of greatest consequence. Other regional efforts will by necessity be broader. For instance, the Indo-Pacific Economic Framework advanced by the United States, but with buy-in from 13 other partners, intends to define regional standards on trade, digital cooperation, supply chains, environmental factors, anti-corruption, and tax policies. Similarly, India's Act East policy is meant in part to integrate more with Southeast Asia and play a supporting role in a broader region including the South Pacific. Meanwhile, more global efforts will require cooperation with extra-regional partners, such as the European Union on many matters of standards and regulations. Furthermore, there are areas where other specific actors outside the Quad—such as France, the United Kingdom, Indonesia, South Korea, and Canada—bring certain competitive advantages to the table. For all these reasons, the Quad is likely to remain one of many parallel efforts to strengthen the emerging international order in the Indo-Pacific.

Multiple Building Blocks

China's growing assertiveness as a single party state, a non-market economy, and a revisionist power has had a transformative effect on the balance of power in the Indo-Pacific and on the broader international order.[19] It ought to be no surprise that India—another large and rising Asian power—should feel the effects. Many of China's efforts have undermined both the international order and Indian security and well-being: anti-satellite tests at high altitudes, the proliferation of weapons of mass destruction, artificial island building in the South China Sea, non-market trade practices, and unsustainable and non-transparent lending.[20] India has had to respond by more actively building up its own capabilities, stepping up in its neighborhood,

---

[18] "Fact Sheet: Quad Leaders' Tokyo Summit 2022," The White House (May 23, 2022).

[19] Doshi (2022).

[20] Broad and Sanger (2007), Hannas et al. (2013), Hayton (2014), Small (2015).

contributing to a stable balance of power in the Indo-Pacific, and representing itself in institutions of global governance.[21]

Partnerships with the industrialized democracies in North America, Europe, and Northeast Asia are critical, and several efforts are likely to proceed in parallel. One is the Quad, which brings together the four most capable and willing partners in the Indo-Pacific. A second is a series of issue-specific middle power coalitions involving France, Indonesia, Japan, Australia, and possibly others. All share different degrees of anxiety about the United States' staying power but have different priorities. Finally, India will on some issues engage directly with the European Union and bilaterally with the United States and Japan as large and capable economies that can contribute to India's internal balancing. This could conceivably extend to trade, investment, development cooperation, and technology partnerships.

All these lines of efforts will strengthen the building blocks necessary to uphold an international order already under immense strain. A more capable India will have greater resources to share the burden in such efforts, which remains very much part of the logic of the Quad. Bilateral relations will over time build habits of cooperation and trust with partners, particularly on sensitive issues and technologies. Ultimately, however, it will come down to leveraging these partnerships to strengthen and update international institutions and norms. Whatever the precise operating definition of the international order, the objectives would broadly be to preserve security and a stable balance of power against territorial revisionism and weapons proliferation; facilitate fair and equitable international commerce; and ensure the responsible and transparent governance of the global commons.

At the same time, there are reasons for caution. India will have misgivings about compromising its own sovereignty. It will insist on more equitable economic and trade terms to allow its still developing economy to compete in the global marketplace. It will also argue for a greater voice and vote for itself at the global high table. And it will support the perspectives of the Global South, in part motivated by concern about China's growing influence in Asia, Africa, the Middle East and Latin America. If these considerations can be kept in mind and sufficiently navigated, it would certainly benefit India's partners in the developed democratic world.

References

Akbaruddin, S. (2021). *India vs UK: The story of an unprecedented diplomatic win*. Harper Collins

Arakkal, S. (2021). *The Australia-India economic relationship: New strategies, new objectives*. Perth US-Asia Centre.

Basrur, R., & Kutty, S. N. (Eds.). (2018). *India and Japan: Assessing the strategic partnership*. Palgrave Pivot.

Bhagavan (Ed.). (2019). *India and the cold war.* UNC Press.

Broad, W. J., & Sanger, D. (2007). China tests anti-satellite weapon, unnerving U.S. *The New York Times*.

---

[21] Jaishankar (2019).

Doshi, R. (2022). *The long game: China's grand strategy to displace American order*. Oxford University Press.
Engerman, D. C. (2018). *The price of aid: The economic cold war in India*. Harvard University Press.
Flitton, D. (2020). Who really killed quad 1.0? *The Interpreter*. Lowy Institute for International Policy.
Hayton, B. (2014). *The South China Sea: The struggle for power in Asia*. Yale University Press.
Hannas, W. C., Mulvenon, J., & Puglisi, A. B. (2013). *China's industrial espionage: Technology acquisition and military modernisation*. Routledge.
Jha, V. (2021). India's moment in the sun: Inside the making of the international solar alliance. JSD Dissertation, Stanford University School of Law.
Jaishankar, D. (2019). *Acting East: India in the Indo-Pacific*. Brookings India.
Jaishankar, D. (2020a). *For India, autarky is not an option*. Observer Research Foundation.
Jaishankar, D. (2020b). *The Australia-India strategic partnership: Accelerating security cooperation*. Lowy Institute for International Policy.
Jaishankar, D., & Madan, T. (2021). How the quad can match the hype. *Foreign Affairs*.
Jaishankar, D., & Madan, T. (2022). The quad needs a harder edge. *Foreign Affairs*.
Modi, N. (2018). *Prime Minister's Speech at Shangri-La Dialogue*. Ministry of External Affairs, Government of India.
Madan, T. (2020a). *What you need to know about the 'quad' in charts," order from chaos*. The Brookings Institution.
Madan, T. (2020b). *Fateful triangle: How China shaped U.S.-India relations during the cold war*. Brookings Institution Press.
Puri, H. S. (2016). *Perilous interventions: The security council and the politics of chaos*. Harper Collins.
Raghavan, S. (2016). When Indian troops entered Congo 55 years ago. *Mint*.
Rajadhyaksha, N. (2019). How India made its mark at the Bretton Woods Conference. *Mint*.
Rehman, I. (2017). *India, China, and differing conceptions of the maritime order*. The Brookings Institution.
Small, A. (2015). *The China-Pakistan axis: Asia's new geopoltiics*. Oxford University Press.
Singh, Z. D. (2019). *Power and diplomacy: Indian foreign policies during the cold war*. Oxford University Press.
Talbott, S. (2004). *Engaging India: Diplomacy, democracy and the bomb*. Brookings Institution Press.
Thakkar, C. (2021). Overcoming the Diego Garcia stalemate. *War on the Rocks*.

Open Access This chapter is licensed under the terms of the Creative Commons Attribution-NonCommercial-NoDerivatives 4.0 International License (http://creativecommons.org/licenses/by-nc-nd/4.0/), which permits any noncommercial use, sharing, distribution and reproduction in any medium or format, as long as you give appropriate credit to the original author(s) and the source, provide a link to the Creative Commons license and indicate if you modified the licensed material. You do not have permission under this license to share adapted material derived from this chapter or parts of it.

The images or other third party material in this chapter are included in the chapter's Creative Commons license, unless indicated otherwise in a credit line to the material. If material is not included in the chapter's Creative Commons license and your intended use is not permitted by statutory regulation or exceeds the permitted use, you will need to obtain permission directly from the copyright holder.

.

Chapter 8
Countering Chinese Economic Coercion and Corrosive Capital in Southeast Asia

Nithin Coca

Abstract Southeast Asian nations, at this point, are unable or unwilling to take an active role in protecting the rules-based liberal international order (LIO) from China-led threats, including territorial disputes. They prioritize economic growth and trade over security or geopolitical concerns, and are not willing to put their economy at risk. Southeast Asian nations are willing to accept Chinese investment because, with the exception of Japan which counters China's Belt and Road Initiative (BRI) in aiding infrastructure and energy projects, there is not a viable alternative. The threat of Chinese economic coercion and fear of losing a key export market run high. Europe and America have mostly withdrawn from investing in Southeast Asia, but the EU's Globally Connected Europe and the U.S.-led Build Back Better World initiative in 2021 provide hope. A joint U.S.-Europe-Japan-led alternative to the BRI can create new standards for transparency, along with clear mechanisms for fair arbitration, debt financing, and judicial processes. A clearer link between the rules and institutions underpinning the LIO and economic growth needs to be shown.

To outside observers, the fact that Southeast Asia is not up in arms about China's rise seems like a paradox. Despite active, militaristic encroachments into Vietnam, Philippines, Indonesia, Malaysia and Brunei's territorial waters and, sometimes, airspace, all these countries are welcoming Chinese investment, including into sensitive sectors such as transportation, technology, and ports.[1] Similarly, China's building of massive dams and limited data sharing along its part of the Mekong River[2]—the lifeblood and source of food for millions in Thailand, Cambodia, and Vietnam, and which is seeing dangerously low flows due to over-development —has not led to any major geopolitical repercussions. How can China get away with this?

---

[1] Josoh (2018).
[2] Citowicki (2020).

N. Coca (✉)
Freelance Journalist and Curator of Asia Undercovered, New York, NY, United States
e-mail: journalism@mail.nithincoca.com

The reason? The economy. Despite China's growing security threats, Southeast Asian nations are willing to accept Chinese investment because, with the exception of Japan, there is not a viable alternative to meet growing energy and infrastructure needs. Moreover, the threat of Chinese economic coercion, as recently experienced by Australia, leaves countries reticent to risk losing not only investments, but a key export market for palm oil, coal, natural gas, agricultural goods, and other commodities.

In short, Southeast Asia is, at this point, unable or unwilling to take an active role in protecting the rules-based liberal international order (LIO) from China-led threats. This has the effect of allowing China to weaken the rules, norms, and institutions that underpin the LIO, including the Association of Southeast Asian Nations (ASEAN), which is increasingly unable to address issues like maritime security, owing to stonewalling by members like Cambodia[3] which has blocked joint-ASEAN action on China's maritime incursions.[4] This is worrying due to Southeast Asia's position at the center of the Indo-Pacific and numerous key trading routes. Creating mechanisms to counter Chinese corrosive capital, including the Belt & Road Initiative (BRI), will be key in countering Chinese influence in the region, and the threat this holds for the LIO.

The BRI and Corrosive Capital

The rise of China has transformed Southeast Asia in ways that few could have imagined at the turn of the millennium. In less than two decades, China has grown to become the main trading partner and investor in Southeast Asia, through efforts such as the BRI.[5] It's a major shift for the region—made of more than 600 million people living in countries that range from highly developed Singapore to undeveloped Laos—which, since the advent of colonialism in the sixteenth century, has been dependent on Europe, America, and Japan.

In fact, it was only in the 1980s and 90 s that Southeast Asia was finally making progress, albeit uneven, around democratization, human rights, and economic growth. Moreover, the main regional organization—ASEAN, the Association of Southeast Asian Nations, initially formed by the region's capitalist countries as a counter to Chinese-led Communist influence, expanded and began to take a more active role in trade, economic, and even maritime policy. There were hopes that it could do for Southeast Asia what the European Union (EU) had done for Europe, linking the region together economically and allowing it to become a more active global player.[6] In fact, according to John J. Mearsheimer, the post-Cold War LIO relied on spreading democracy around the world, leading to the risk of competing

---

[3] Bokarev (2017).
[4] Blanchard et al. (2016).
[5] Zoltai and Klemensits (2020).
[6] Mahbubani and Thompson (2014).

U.S. and China-led "bounding orders."[7] Southeast Asia is, in many ways, a key space of contestation between these competing orders.

The link between economic growth, trade, and democratization even made Southeast Asia seem like a potential case study for liberalism theory—the idea that economic development would lead to less conflict, increased democratization and more civil and political rights.[8] This theory was also used to argue in favor of China's ascension to the World Trade Organization and other global institutions, or countries like the United States offering preferred trade status to authoritarian countries.

Since then, however, that optimism has faded, and democratic progress has stalled.[9] While this started, perhaps, with the Asian Financial Crisis of 1997–1999, which impacted the region heavily and led to decreased trust of global institutions like the World Bank and International Monetary Fund, the key factor has been the rise of China and the growth of Chinese-led corrosive capital into the region.

According to the Center for International Private Enterprise,[10] "corrosive capital" is "state-backed financing that lacks transparency and accountability flowing from authoritarian states into new and fragile democracies." For Southeast Asia, China is the preeminent source of corrosive capital, which often flows through opaque channels, and increases "political and economic distortions which often do more harm than good in the recipient country."

While there are many venues and pathways for Chinese corrosive capital to reach Southeast Asia, the one that gets the most attention is the BRI. It was launched in 2013, and from its inception, Southeast Asia has been a focus, and the Maritime Silk Road component was announced by a speech by Premier Xi Jinping in Indonesia.[11] The BRI has funded rail lines in Laos and Malaysia, power plants in Vietnam and Indonesia, ports in Myanmar, roads in Papua New Guinea and East Timor, and much, much more. For the most part, the financing of these projects is mostly secretive, likely by design, with the best estimates putting the total BRI figure in Southeast Asia at $740 million in 2018. The BRI is rife with concerns. It prioritizes the use of Chinese contractors, imported Chinese labor, and may include onerous terms that could put the country's finances, or patrimonial assets, at risk.

Europe and America Missing—But Not Japan

Alongside China's rise, the past two decades have seen Europe and America mostly withdrawn from investing in infrastructure and energy projects in Southeast Asia. Japan, notably, has not, and Japanese institutions are working on a wide range of energy, rail, and road projects across the region, often competing with, and sometimes

---

[7] Mearsheimer (2019).

[8] McGlinchey and Meiser (n.d.).

[9] Slater (2022).

[10] Center for International Private Enterprise (2020).

[11] Synergia Foundation (2019).

beating, rival Chinese-led projects. But while Japan has offered Southeast Asia an alternative choice to China's BRI, it hasn't offered an alternative model.

Moreover, Japan has been willing to invest in countries that have been actively enabling China's weakening of the LIO, such as Cambodia. The most egregious example is Myanmar, where, since the 2021 coup, many Japanese companies continue to operate as if business is normal, even as the U.S. and many European nations sanction and limit economic cooperation with the junta government.

Japan cannot be the sole alternative to China, lacking, as it does, the capital and capacity to meet Southeast Asia's infrastructure and investments needs on its own. Europe and America, however, could. Combining Japan's local knowledge and expertise with added capital and technology could provide a far more viable alternative to the BRI. There is momentum here as understanding of the BRI's geopolitical implications grows, including the announcement of the U.S.-led Build Back Better World' (B3W) initiative in 2021, shortly after the European Union unveiled its own effort, Globally Connected Europe. How they integrate and are designed will be critical in determining whether they can counter the BRI's corrosive impact.

There is an opportunity here because, while the BRI has been appealing, particularly to authoritarian-minded governments,[12] it has been beset with political and logistical challenges. The use of Chinese labor versus local workers has become a point of contention in Indonesia and the Philippines.[13] One of the premier projects in the region, the Jakarta-Bandung High Speed Rail line, has been beset with delays due to faulty land acquisition, flooding, and cost overruns. And in Malaysia, concerns about unfair financing became a political issue during the 2018 election, which resulted in the new government canceling a railway project and re-negotiating its terms.[14]

A joint, U.S.-Europe-Japan-led BRI alternative can avoid these issues by creating new standards for transparency, along with clear mechanisms for fair arbitration, debt financing, and judicial processes. They should be multilateral and build on existing international institutions and frameworks, such as the Paris Club, created in 1956, a platform for coordinated and sustainable solutions to the payment difficulties experienced by debtor countries. The U.S., most of the EU, and Japan are members; China is not, and China's BRI deals, in stark contrast, are mostly secretive, and the few that have been public have worrying clauses, including ones that force recipient countries to conduct arbitration in Chinese courts.[15]

Trade could also be used as a tool. According to data from the Organisation for Economic Cooperation (OECD) China is the largest trading partner with several Southeast Asian nations. But if you combine the U.S, Japan and Europe, together they dwarf China. The key difference is that, unlike other countries, China has shown a willingness to use trade as an economic tool, violating the spirit if not the clauses of the trade agreements and institutions it is a member of.

---

[12] Camba (2021).

[13] Tippett and Hillman (2021).

[14] Ng (2019).

[15] Wooley (2021).

Southeast Asia watched closely when China blocked imports of Australian coal, wine, and other goods in response to its call for an independent inquiry into the origins of the COVID-19 pandemic.[16] In many cases this benefited countries in the region, like Indonesia, who saw coal exports to China rise. It was also notable how Australia's allies in Europe and America were only willing to call China out politically, but were happy to meet Chinese demand for banned Australian agricultural exports such as wood and wine.[17]

In this case, fighting fire with fire—threatening economic coercion—is not the right option. Instead, the U.S., Japan, and Europe should work to strengthen the ability of the rules-based LIO so as to counter the threat of Chinese economic coercion. There are many ways this could be done. Reforming the World Trade Organization, which has not been able to adequately respond to China's tactics, is one option, while new trade agreements that better recognize and account for this threat are another.

Creating trade mechanisms that reduce the risk of economic coercion could be appealing to Southeast Asian economies, which are, for the most part, unable to risk being cut off from Chinese markets like Australia was. Responses to Chinese coercion need to be stronger and more effective. The U.S. or Japan should not be benefiting from China's unfair trade barriers against Australia; instead, they need to respond with shows of solidarity. This will be even more important if and when a Southeast Asian nation is threatened by economic coercion. Only by reducing this threat can space be made for broader cooperation on security or geopolitical issues, including in the Indo-Pacific.

Geoeconomics Before Security

When considering the turmoil and conflict cause by western and Japanese influence in the region, such as the Vietnam War, or the United States-supported 1965 Indonesia coup, it is hard to argue that Southeast Asia has benefited or really been an active participant in either the Cold War or post-Cold War rules-based liberal international order.

Part of this is just a reflection of the region, and the fact that different countries have differing goals, particularly when it comes to security or geopolitics. But if there is one thing that the 10 member nations of ASEAN, with their diverse ethnic, religious, development, and political make-up, have in common, it is this. They prioritize economic growth, trade, and the creation of wealth, over security or geopolitical concerns, and they are not willing to take positions that put their economy at risk. This applies to China, but also Russia, as, besides Singapore, no ASEAN nation has joined the western-backed sanctions regime over the invasion of Ukraine.

This is why the focus on security issues around China's expanded military presence in the South China Sea has been limited because, to most Southeast Asia nations,

---

[16] Glaser (2021).

[17] Tan (2021).

economic security is often of greater importance. Providing a way to counter the threat of Chinese economic coercion and providing an investment alternative to the BRI would give more space for security cooperation in the region as well.

To do this, there needs to be a greater understanding that trade and investment alone does not necessarily lead to democratization, a stronger liberal international order, or a more effective ASEAN. There needs to be a direct connection between the rules and institutions that underpin the LIO and the combat against the risk of Chinese corrosive capital in the region. That means better cooperation between Europe, the U.S., and Japan on creating not just an alternative choice to the BRI, but an alternative model that can help rebuild the relationship between economic growth and liberalism, and allow Southeast Asia the choice not to be trapped in China's growing shadow, in perpetual fear of economic coercion.

References

Blanchard, B., Martina, M., & Mogato, M. (2016). ASEAN deadlocked on South China Sea, Cambodia blocks statement. *Reuters*. https://www.reuters.com/article/us-southchinasea-ruling-asean-idUSKCN1050F6

Bokarev, D. (2017). Cambodia as an example of Chinese influence in ASEAN. *New Eastern Outlook*. https://journal-neo.org/2017/01/10/cambodia-as-an-example-of-chinese-influence-in-asean/

Camba, A. (2021). How Chinese firms approach investment risk: Strong leaders, cancellation, and pushback. *Review of International Political Economy* (2021). https://www.tandfonline.com/doi/full/https://doi.org/10.1080/09692290.2021.1947345.

Center for International Private Enterprise. (2020) Mitigating governance risks from investment in Southeast Asia. https://www.cipe.org/wp-content/uploads/2020/04/MXW_CIPE_ChinaReport_20200521_Overview.pdf

Citowicki, P. (2020). China's control of the Mekong. *The Diplomat*. https://thediplomat.com/2020/05/chinas-control-of-the-mekong/

Glaser, B. S. (2021). Time for collective pushback against China's economic coercion. *Commentary by the Center for Strategic and International Studies*. https://www.csis.org/analysis/time-collective-pushback-against-chinas-economic-coercion

Josoh, S. (2018). *The Impact of BRI on trade and investment in ASEAN. China's belt and road initiative and Southeast Asia*. CIMB ASEAN Research Institute.

Mahbubani, K., & Thompson, F. (2014). Unlocking ASEAN's potential. *Project Syndicate*. https://www.project-syndicate.org/commentary/southeast-asia-economic-open-market-by-kishore-mahbubani-and-fraser-thompson-2014-12

McGlinchey, S., & Meiser, J. W. (n.d.). International relations theory. https://www.e-ir.info/publication/international-relations-theory/

Mearsheimer, J. J. (2019). Bound to fail: The rise and fall of the liberal international order. *International Security 43*(4).

Ng, E. (2019). Malaysia: Revised China deal shows costs were inflated. *The Diplomat*. https://thediplomat.com/2019/04/malaysia-revised-china-deal-shows-costs-were-inflated/

Slater, D. (2022). Asia no arc toward wealthy democracy. *East Asia Forum* (2022). https://www.eastasiaforum.org/2022/04/03/asia-no-arc-toward-wealthy-democracy/

Synergia Foundation. (2019). Indonesia and the belt and road initiative. https://www.synergiafoundation.org/insights/analyses-assessments/indonesia-and-belt-and-road-initiative

Tan, S.-L. (2021). *US exports to China grow at 'expense' of Australia after Beijing's trade ban. South China morning post sec.* China Macro Economy. https://www.scmp.com/economy/global-economy/article/3133952/us-exports-china-grow-expense-australia-after-beijings-trade

Tippett, A., & Hillman, J. (2021). Who built that? Labor and the belt and road initiative. (blog). https://www.cfr.org/blog/who-built-labor-and-belt-and-road-initiative

Wooley, A. (2021). AidData's new dataset of 13,427 Chinese development projects worth $843 billion reveals major increase in 'hidden debt' and belt and road initiative implementation problems. *Aid Data.* https://www.aiddata.org/blog/aiddatas-new-dataset-of-13-427-chinese-development-projects-worth-843-billion-reveals-major-increase-in-hidden-debt-and-belt-and-road-initiative-implementation-problems

Zoltai, A., & Klemensits, P. (2020). What do China and the BRI mean to ASEAN economies? *Foreign Policy Review.*

Open Access This chapter is licensed under the terms of the Creative Commons Attribution-NonCommercial-NoDerivatives 4.0 International License (http://creativecommons.org/licenses/by-nc-nd/4.0/), which permits any noncommercial use, sharing, distribution and reproduction in any medium or format, as long as you give appropriate credit to the original author(s) and the source, provide a link to the Creative Commons license and indicate if you modified the licensed material. You do not have permission under this license to share adapted material derived from this chapter or parts of it.

The images or other third party material in this chapter are included in the chapter's Creative Commons license, unless indicated otherwise in a credit line to the material. If material is not included in the chapter's Creative Commons license and your intended use is not permitted by statutory regulation or exceeds the permitted use, you will need to obtain permission directly from the copyright holder.

Chapter 9
The Challenge of China for the Liberal International Order

Richard McGregor

Abstract China is willing to talk about the "rules-based order" by crowning it with the skeptical term "so-called," thus criticizing it as a system established by the U.S. for the ultimate benefit of the U.S. and its allies. Beijing thinks the global system must be modified to suit their interests, or otherwise it will conspire against them and corrode their grip on power at home. The country has benefited more than anyone from the post-Cold War liberalization of the economic order. While downplaying human rights, democracy and shared values, China attempts to set global rules at the UN on international economy and finance, regional cooperation, and emerging areas such as the oceans, the poles, cyberspace, and outer space, and, where it sees further chances, launch rival or parallel bodies—the Asian Infrastructure Investment Bank, the Shanghai Co-operation Organisation, and the BRICS, for example. Beijing had once accommodated the rules-based order, but now it feels that the rules-based order must accommodate China.

How do the Chinese party-state and its most senior officials think about the rule-based international order?

Yang Jiechi, Beijing's top diplomat and Politburo member, delivered China's definitive view on the concept at his first meeting with senior members of the Biden administration in Alaska, in March 2021.[1]

On the Chinese Internet, the sharpest parts of the lengthy and now infamous diatribe delivered by Yang in Alaska, directed across the table at Anthony Blinken, the Secretary of State, and Jake Sullivan, the National Security Adviser, went viral.

In China, street vendors drummed up a brisk trade almost overnight selling T-shirts and tea mugs adorned with his words about how America should "stop interfering in China's internal affairs" and so forth.

---

[1] U.S. Department of State (2021).

R. McGregor (✉)
Lowy Institute, Sydney, Australia

© The International House of Japan, Inc. 2024
Y. Hosoya and H. Kundnani (eds.), *The Transformation of the Liberal International Order*, SpringerBriefs in International Relations,
https://doi.org/10.1007/978-981-99-4729-4_9

But the substance of Yang's exposition lay elsewhere and was not destined to gain transitory fame as a meme.

Unprompted by his American interlocutors, Yang enunciated how Beijing believed the world should be ordered, and how its viewpoint differed from that of the United States.

China's focus, Yang said, was on what he called the United Nations-centered international system, underlined by international law. The "so-called" rules-based order led by the U.S., by contrast, he said, was only followed by a "small number of countries."

Beijing has a habit of attaching the adjective "so-called" to concepts or ideas when it aims to denigrate them. Its spokesmen often refer to America's "so-called" democracy; they call the four-country grouping of the U.S., Japan, India and Australia the "so-called Quad" and they disparage western efforts to investigate human rights atrocities in Xinjiang by referring to the "so-called Uyghur tribunal."

China's objections to the "so-called rules-based order" run wide and deep, and across institutions and continents, but they can also be summed up simply. China believes that that rules-based system was established by the U.S. for the ultimate benefit of the U.S., and its allies.

U.S.-China competition covers multiple domains—military, trade, geopolitics, technology and so forth. But increasingly, especially through Beijing's eyes, it is a contest of political systems, in which the party-state is constantly defending itself against attacks from western democracies.

Once that it understood, it is not hard to see how Beijing has concluded that the global system must be modified to suit their interests. Otherwise, it will inevitably conspire against them and corrode their grip on power at home.

As Yang said in Alaska: "The overwhelming majority of countries in the world would recognize that the universal values advocated by the United States or that the opinion of the United States could represent international public opinion."[2]

> Those countries would not recognize that the rules made by a small number of people would serve as the basis for the international order.

In other words, in rejecting the rules-based order, China—and other countries—are also rejecting universal values, at least as propagated by the West and its allies.

As one of the T-shirts printed after the Alaska meeting said, the U.S. cannot speak for China, nor for any other countries around the world.

It is not clear whether Yang's use of the phrase "rules-based order," instead of another term more favored in the U.S., "liberal international order," was significant in any fashion. Whatever the distinction between the two, they are generally used interchangeably in foreign policy circles.

Many scholars, and not just in China, have long criticized the rubberiness and ambiguity of the concept of the post-war liberal order.

---

[2] Ibid (xxxx).

Graham Allison, of Harvard University, for example, says proponents of the "liberal order" credit it with the long peace between the major powers after World War II.[3]

"But the 'long peace' was not the result of the liberal order, but the by-product of the dangerous balance of power between the Soviet Union and the U.S. during the four and a half decades of the Cold War, and then a brief period of U.S. dominance," says Allison.

Still, both the U.S. and China at the very least accept the existence of a rule-based order, and the two countries agree that it has been a dominant force in global politics since the end of the war.

Chinese scholars also acknowledge that the international post-war order, at least once Beijing opted in after the reform-and-opening period from 1979 onwards, was beneficial in many ways for China.

Wu Xinbo, of Fudan University, in Shanghai, in an article for the Lowy Institute, said that China held a significant stake in the existing order, and, by and large, favored its preservation.[4]

But Beijing also desired to reform the order, he said, as an important qualification, so as to better accommodate its own interests and preferences.

In other words, China is not going to overturn the current order or create a new one, but it will drive the order's evolution and adaption in a fast-changing world. On the face of it, this position sounds positive.

How does China benefit? In Dr. Wu's words, China enjoys special standing as a permanent member of the United Nations Security Council and its economy is now the world's second-largest economy, thanks to an open international economic system.

On the security front, since the end of the Cold War, China has not been confronted with a major external military threat and has benefited from an overall peaceful international environment.

In the 1980s, when China's economy started to take off in the first wave of reform, Deng Xiaoping refused to divert scarce resources to the military, effectively contracting out security in the Asia–Pacific to the nearby American forces.

But that was never going to last. Beijing has always harbored deep reservations about the liberal order because of its American roots.

In an era of superpower competition, such qualities render it immediately suspect, as other countries, especially ones which are not U.S. allies, will always occupy a lesser position in that order.

For Beijing which considers itself to be on a par with the U.S., that is not good enough. It wants a status commensurate with its growing power in major international economic and financial institutions.

Once China was willing to accommodate the rules-based order. Now the rules-based order must accommodate China. Inevitably, that meant a powerful China would challenge the U.S. and the rules-based order when it was able to do so.

---

[3] Graham Allison (2023).
[4] Wu Xinbo (2023).

In terms of pure power politics, with its economy approaching that of the U.S. in aggregate size and its military rapidly expanding, China can mount a strong argument that the old ways will not work anymore.

Much of the surviving rhetoric in western capitals assumes that Washington retains the luxury of deciding whether it would like to strike a deal with Beijing.

In truth, Beijing has been making the running in re-fashioning the world, and Washington is only now starting to catch up.

Beijing also argues that the current order does not address major global challenges and thus should not stand in the way of needed reform and adjustments. In that respect, Beijing says it is not detracting from the current order. Rather it is helping to strengthen the order and widen its ambit to make it more effective.

After all, throughout history, the global order has never been static. It has evolved constantly to meet new challenges and adapt to changing realities.

As Donald Trump has reminded the world, the threat to current order might not come from China anyway, but from the U.S. Any U.S. president could walk away from it, as Mr Trump constantly threatened to do.

The sorts of reforms and changes put forward by the likes of Dr Wu, of Fudan University—for China to have a seat at the table and for its security concerns to be respected—again sound reasonable enough on the surface.

Some of Beijing's complaints are in fact reasonable. Given the size of its economy, China can rightly argue that it should have a bigger role and shareholding in archetypal post-war institutions like the World Bank and the International Monetary Fund.

But China's changes are in fact quite radical on many levels. Consider the United Nations. Over more than a decade, Beijing has remorselessly chipped away at the definition of universal human rights.

In place of the founding ethos, China wants the definition to reflect its own governing values, with a focus not on political rights but economic opportunities—a radical change.

The changes to the current order that China insists on include an acknowledgement of its security, which includes unification with Taiwan, and command over the South China Sea.

Once these demands are taken into account, China's stated position—of China adapting to the rules-based order and vice versa—looks a lot less benign, and much more dramatic and disruptive.

Once you accede to Beijing's demands in the South China Sea, you are effectively unravelling the entirety of what we call the San Francisco System—the web of agreements covering the region struck in the wake of the war.

Most discussions about the rules-based order focus on competition between the U.S. and China. But in the South China Sea, China's claims cut across those of multiple other smaller countries.

China's security demands also include bringing Taiwan, a thriving democracy of 26 million people who have no desire to be ruled from Beijing, under its sovereignty.

Once again, this amounts to a radical rewriting of the rules, and the upending of the region which will be forced not just to acknowledge Chinese power but also to accommodate its core demands.

Thus far, in setting global rules, China has focused on the United Nations, international economy and finance, regional cooperation, and emerging areas such as the oceans, the poles, cyberspace, and outer space.

Beijing has also been an aggressive setter of new technology standards, largely through the Belt & Road Initiative and initiatives like Huawei's smart cities in Africa and the Middle East.

On top of playing the game in existing institutions, China has pursued a strategy of establishing rival or parallel bodies in areas where it feels underrepresented, or where it sees a gap in the market.

There is already a plethora of them—the Asian Infrastructure Investment Bank, the Shanghai Co-operation Organisation, the BRICS grouping, consisting of China, Russia, Brazil, India and South Africa, and the "17 + 1" arrangement in Europe.

These parallel institutions can thrive and in doing so corrode the legitimacy of existing bodies, as the Asian Infrastructure Investment Bank (AIIB) is doing with the Japan-led Asia Development Bank.

Alternatively, they can lie fallow, only to be revived at politically opportune moments, as in the case of BRICS, which is getting fresh life after Russia's invasion of Ukraine.

At the same time, China is joining regional agreements where its suits its interests. For example, it was one of the key partners in negotiating the Regional Economic Comprehensive Partnership (RCEP). It has also signalled its desire to join the revamped version of the Trans-Pacific Partnership, which had threatened to fall apart when the U.S. dropped out.

Over time, however, if its economy continues to develop and its military power expands, Beijing will expect to be much more of a rule-setter than a rule-taker.

In Xi Jinping's own words, the task of the party and its leaders is to "lay the foundation for a future where we will win the initiative and have the dominant position."

That does not mean that China will try to export its own model to other countries.

A lot of sloppy analysis about China "exporting its model" misses the point—that the China model, which combines a centuries-old bureaucratic culture with a Leninist structure imported from the Soviet Union, is neither replicable elsewhere, nor fit for purpose in other countries.

Beijing is self-aware enough to know that other countries cannot structure their governments along its exact same lines.

Just as democracy in the United States looks very different from democracies in other countries, China's authoritarian system does not fit neatly within the administrations of other non-democratic states.

But if China cannot export its model lock, stock, and barrel, it is already exporting segments of it in ways that extend its influence, in both governance and technological standards.

That means that China will set and export technological standards, and political values, and the rules that go with them. Over time, China will talk less about the benefits of the current rules-based order, and more about its own rules. That by itself, marks a seismic shift in the global order.

References

Graham Allison, The Truth About the Liberal Order: Why It Didn't Make the Modern World (August 28, 2018). https://www.foreignaffairs.com/united-states/truth-about-liberal-order. Accessed on April 21, 2023.
Ibid (xxxx).
U.S. Department of State, "Secretary Antony J. Blinken, National Security Advisor Jake Sullivan, Director Yang And State Councilor Wang At the Top of Their Meeting" (March 18, 2021). https://www.state.gov/secretary-antony-j-blinken-national-security-advisor-jake-sullivan-chinese-director-of-the-office-of-the-central-commission-for-foreign-affairs-yang-jiechi-and-chinese-state-councilor-wang-yi-at-th/. Accessed on April 21, 2023.
Wu Xinbo, Can Washington compromise? (28 October 2020). https://interactives.lowyinstitute.org/features/china-rules-based-order/articles/can-washington-compromise/. Accessed on April 21, 2023.

Open Access This chapter is licensed under the terms of the Creative Commons Attribution-NonCommercial-NoDerivatives 4.0 International License (http://creativecommons.org/licenses/by-nc-nd/4.0/), which permits any noncommercial use, sharing, distribution and reproduction in any medium or format, as long as you give appropriate credit to the original author(s) and the source, provide a link to the Creative Commons license and indicate if you modified the licensed material. You do not have permission under this license to share adapted material derived from this chapter or parts of it.

The images or other third party material in this chapter are included in the chapter's Creative Commons license, unless indicated otherwise in a credit line to the material. If material is not included in the chapter's Creative Commons license and your intended use is not permitted by statutory regulation or exceeds the permitted use, you will need to obtain permission directly from the copyright holder.

Chapter 10
Northeast Asia's Energy Transition–Challenges for a Rules-Based Security and Economic Order

Kun-Chin Lin and Tim Reilly

Abstract Would the rise and political convergence of a dominant gas supplier (Russia) and an outsized consumer (the People's Republic of China) prohibit or facilitate the rise of multilateral energy governance in Northeast Asia? We revisit conventional views on challenges to interstate cooperation on managing energy demand and related infrastructure provision among Japan, South Korea (ROK), and the People's Republic of China. Through a "geoeconomic" analysis that tracks the interplay between national energy transition and the securitization of energy policies, we suggest that Northeast Asia energy interdependence relations are in the process of being drawn into a Eurasian Arctic and heartland framework that mediates great power competition across energy, financial, and diplomatic domains. Against these pressures, Japan, the European Union and the U.S. would need to reconceptualize the geographical basis of a regional liberal institutional order as defined in this book.

Introduction: Energy Transition and Energy Security in Northeast Asia Since the Asian Financial Crisis[1]

This chapter proposes an original perspective on multilateral energy governance in Northeast Asia, aiming to overcome the long acknowledged and studied problems with interstate cooperation on and institutionalization of collective management of energy demand and related infrastructure provision among Japan, South Korea

---

[1] We are grateful to organizers and participants of the API preparatory workshops, and Ariana Zarrabian for the able research assistance.

K.-C. Lin (✉)
Department of Spacepower, Air University, Maxwell Airforce Base, Montgomery, AL, US

Paul H. Nitze School of Advanced International Studies, Johns Hopkins University, Washington D.C., US

T. Reilly
Scott Polar Research Institute, University of Cambridge, Cambridge, UK

(ROK), and the People's Republic of China (PRC) as major fossil fuel consumers. We provide a "geoeconomic" analysis that tracks the interplay between national energy transition and the securitization of energy policies and suggest that coordinated policies that bring together a mix of market mechanisms and government-supported (although not necessarily interstate) institutionalization could address the structural needs of these countries in a way that is consistent with the paradigm of a regional liberal institutional order as defined in this book.

The first section below summarizes conventional explanations for a lack of impetus toward collective energy security in Northeast Asia, despite expert proposals that reflect tangible national benefits from cooperation. The second section updates market trends and strategic responses from governments, corporate and social interests. The third section suggests pathways to cooperation and possible scenarios of geopolitical polarization of energy policies. We conclude by extending our basic analysis to consider the unfolding impact of Russian invasion of Ukraine in 2022 on Eurasian energy geoeconomics, in particular how fossil fuel markets will be realigned and whether renewables, including the highly touted green/blue hydrogen technologies, could affect fundamental incentives for regional cooperation.

A. Northeast Asian energy cooperation since the late-1990s.

The Asian Financial Crisis and its immediate aftermath of 1997–9 denote a significant shift in national energy policies and politics in Northeast Asia. While Japan and ROK saw reductions from previously rapid increases in oil consumption and import, PRC experienced a rapid growth in dependence on imported crude oil as its basic energy policy shifted from one of conservation and maximization of domestic deposits to one of diversification of suppliers.[2] The shift in Japan and ROK coincided with increasing global awareness of the environmental, social, and commercial issues associated with hydrocarbon consumption, including negative experiences such as the staggering growth of Chinese coal-burning power stations and their associated transborder health and pollution problems, as well as positive ones such as emerging technologies like liquefied natural gas (LNG) and solar panels, which provide the bases for a region-wide energy transition. The culmination of the UN Framework Convention on Climate Change (UNFCCC) COP discussions in Paris 2015 prompted countries to provide roadmaps toward substantial climate change mitigation, with Japan and Korea pledging carbon neutrality by 2050 and China aiming to peak its carbon emissions by 2030.[3] Paris 2015 also marked a geopolitical emergence of a "G2" arrangement in climate change cooperation and policy coordination between the U.S. and the PRC, with distinctively different philosophies driving long-term policy orientations. While President Obama emphasized "mitigation" measures to contain and reverse environmental damages, such as preventative policies, regulations, climate investigation, and the promotion of multilateralism in

---

[2] Thorarinsson (2018), Calder (2005), Guy et al. (2011).

[3] https://sdg.iisd.org/news/japan-republic-of-korea-pledge-to-go-carbon-neutral-by-2050/; https://www4.unfccc.int/sites/ndcstaging/PublishedDocuments/China%20First/China%E2%80%99s%20Achievements,%20New%20Goals%20and%20New%20Measures%20for%20Nationally%20Determined%20Contributions.pdf.

international forums, his Russian and Chinese counterparts have leaned on "adaptation" strategies that attempt to downplay threats and reveal new geographical spaces and economic opportunities in the changing environment. Their viewpoint has translated into building urban and transport infrastructure, investing in new energy technologies, and forging geopolitical alliances to exploit the melting Arctic's Northern Sea Route as a new global trade route linking the East to the West. One could argue that the one-term U.S. President Donald Trump interpreted climate change in terms of a pivotal geopolitical threat, and also as an opportunity, as he offered abundant American shale oil and gas abroad as a means of his politically heightened and securitized foreign policy. As a result, Russia, China, and other countries have become sensitized to the "weaponization" of environmental energy policies, commercial issues such as icebreakers and Liquified Natural Gas (LNG) transportation via the Northern Sea Route (NSR), and the International Maritime Organization's formulation—per Arctic Council's commission—of the NSR's Polar Code for maritime movement along its course.[4]

One might expect that the regional thirst for natural gas, the collective goods of climate change mitigation, clean energy technological advances, the rising importance of LNG relative to pipeline gas, and the overall shift in global economic gravity from the mid-Atlantic to Asia would have led to greater Northeast Asian energy cooperation. Yet for the past two decades, Northeast Asia (NEA) countries have little to show in terms of multilateral cooperation. At the discourse level, the Trilateral Northeast Asia Summit has periodically issued statements on energy cooperation and energy efficiency goals for sustainable growth and co-prosperity since 2011, and addressed nuclear energy security and risks in the aftermath of Fukushima as well as intentions to strengthen cooperation to enhance the efficiency of LNG market in NEA. There is, however, little evidence to date of concrete steps toward joint policy formulation and implementation. The summit in 2018 focused on geopolitical dilemmas and pan-Asian trade arrangement in the aftermath of U.S. withdrawal from the Trans-Pacific Partnership, and the progress report in 2019 made a passing reference to the G20 Ministerial Meeting on Energy Transitions and Global Environment for Sustainable Growth held in Karuizawa in June 2019 and related G20 initiatives.[5] Taking stock of a broad range of government-private sector activities, Choo found limited cases of energy technology cooperation for the enhancement of energy efficiency and environmental cooperation.[6] The UN sponsors the Economic and Social Commission for Asia and the Pacific-Greater Tumen Initiative Seminar on Energy Cooperation, which have focused discussions on subregional power interconnections to help achieve carbon neutrality through trade in renewables. In 2021, it launched a workshop on the North-East Asia Green Power Corridor Roadmap,

---

[4] As manifested in Secretary of State Mike Pompeo's lambasting of Russia and China at the May 2019 Arctic Council meeting, and criticized Beijing's self-description as a near-Arctic power. https://www.reuters.com/article/us-finland-arctic-council-idUSKCN1SC1AY.

[5] https://www.crisisgroup.org/asia/north-east-asia/trilateral-north-east-asia-summit-signals-return-cooperation; https://www.tcs-asia.org/data/etcData/PUB_1618555301.pdf.

[6] Choo (2016).

which was then picked up by the Asian Development Bank (ADB) and discussed as member states' strategies.[7]

B. Academic and industry perceptions of the potential for cooperation

Political economists have mainly sought to explain why there have not been significant efforts to coordinate energy needs in NEA despite the clear functional benefits of cooperation and managed economic complementarities. Authors in *Northeast Asia: Ripe for Integration?* agreed on several political factors necessary for regionalism to move forward, including: (1) the strength of global institutions such as the World Trade Organization (WTO) and International Monetary Fund (IMF); (2) positivity in the Sino-Japanese relationship; (3) the "balance of interests" between the U.S. and the EU concerning Northeast Asia as their economic and security partner region, with a lack of such intentions likely to lead to an inward-looking East Asian or a China-centered regional hierarchy.[8] Choo points to Russia's unique and powerful position as the dominant regional supplier of oil and gas, which has driven Japan, South Korea and China to cultivate bilateral energy relations.[9] He sees dim prospect for regional cooperation, as "each individual perspective on the issue of cooperation is unilateral (self-centered), bilateral (level of cooperation), omni-directional (all the world energy producers) and multifaceted".[10] The collapse of the Sino-Japanese joint exploration agreement in the East China Sea is a case in point of how a cooperative approach quickly turned into a zero-sum game in which the Japanese commissioned a surveying ship for offshore oil deposits in response to China's alleged drilling of the Chunhao gas fields in the disputed waters.[11] In other words, as long as energy is a "high politics" issue of national security importance, NEA countries' risk management strategies will lead to rivalry and divergence of interests. Implications for unequal economic development as noted above also factor into this zero-sum perception.

In contrast, Carla Freeman (2015) offers a more optimistic view of countries' willingness to act on the advantages of cooperation. She explicitly posits a range of benefits of *openness* through institutionalization, as evidenced in established organizations such as the International Energy Agency (IEA), Gas Exporting Countries Forum, Joint Organisations Data Initiative, Organisation of the Petroleum Exporting Countries, International Partnership for Energy Efficiency Cooperation, and International Renewable Energy Agency. Freeman notes that Asian regional energy forums and nascent institutions already capture some of the benefits, including data sharing, improved communication among consumers and producers, and organizational capabilities to positively socialize members and deliver project financing. ADB-led Central Asia Regional Economic Cooperation program as well as the Greater Mekong

---

[7] https://www.adb.org/sites/default/files/publication/664331/eawp-030-neasia-power-system-interconnection.pdf; https://www.adb.org/projects/48030-001/main.

[8] Aggarwal and Koo, eds. (2008) p. 259.

[9] Choo (2016) p. 92.

[10] Ibid, p. 103.

[11] Schultheiss (2020, 2021).

Subregion have gone further in facilitating transboundary cooperation around energy delivery.[12] Consistent with the long-standing nature of Asian regionalism, these regional energy institutions do not set binding rules or implement interventionist measures such as price stabilization, emergency energy management and regional stockpiling.[13] Despite the current state of "shallow cooperation," Freeman sees an emerging framework in which Russia, PRC, Japan and South Korea can interact and cooperate in energy security.[14] The framework is shaped by security principles such as energy efficiency and transition to renewables, complementary activities such as emergency response measures and data collection and sharing, and increasing connectedness among the four NEA states via global markets.

Transborder electricity grid is a project that has received a lot of attention and promotion by Asian regional institutions, with analysts pointing to the ASEAN Power Grid project as a valuable reference point for NEA's potential development.[15] For example, Yun and Zhang (2005) discussed how China could supply electricity to Southeast Asian neighbors during disruptions.[16] Their optimistic, economically focused view should be tempered by practical considerations of redistributive implications in China, such as reduced energy supply for electricity consuming Guangdong and Sichuan from electricity producing provinces such as Guangxi and Yunnan. If the grid channels energy production in remote regions to consumer centers—e.g., Mongolia to Seoul—it might create new patterns of uneven and unequal development over time. To the extent that the expanded market dynamics of the grid could improve efficiency of energy transactions, it is likely to benefit China as the supplier over more advanced energy markets such as South Korea, and therefore create contentions over relative gains over time. This consideration could be a key reason that the Japanese government has avoided talking about Softbank's proposed Asian Supergrid, as noted by Mika Ohbayashi of the Renewable Energy Institute (REI).[17]

Nonetheless, industry and international organization analysts have touted the potential benefits of the process of working towards a transborder, multinational grid, including improved communication between states, harmonization of laws and regulations, and the establishment of confidence-building measures such as shared monitoring and data collection, and regular negotiation and expanded participation opportunities.[18] The Association of Southeast Asian Nations (ASEAN) Power Grid project has also fostered a transborder epistemic community, backed by governments'

---

[12] Freeman (2015) p. 18.

[13] Aggarwal and Lin (2001).

[14] Freeman (2015) p. 20.

[15] Two major UNESCAP reports are: https://repository.unescap.org/bitstream/handle/20.500.12870/1542/ESCAP-2019-FS-Electricity-connectivity-roadmap-Asia-Pacific.pdf?sequence=1&isAllowed=y; https://www.unescap.org/resources/regional-power-grid-connectivity-sustainable-development-north-east-asia. Korneev and Korneev (2019) make a similar case for the Trans-ASEAN Gas Pipeline project.

[16] Yun and Zhang (2005).

[17] Basu (2019).

[18] Ding et al. (2020).

working relations with policy-influential experts and linked forward to global institutions such as the Paris Agreement of UNFCCC and individual countries' commitment to securing a target ratio of primary energy from renewable sources (IRENA).[19]

Choo points out the paradoxes inherent in regionalism in energy. First, energy security could be attained at the cost of motivation for cooperation, such as if the states have reliable access to cheap oil and gas supplies from a stable group of diverse suppliers.[20] Second, national governments gain political currency in talking about cooperation and openness, when actual policies tend to be protectionist of domestic importers and preferential with suppliers. He observes the vehemence that Chinese and Japanese energy officials have shown rhetorically in advocating regional energy cooperation with Southeast Asian countries.[21] In practice, PRC has shunned cooperation with rivals and instead conducted economic statecraft with energy producers such as Australia, Malaysia and Russia.

C. New themes and key insights from a "geoeconomic" perspective

We argue that the mainstream explanations above miss important dimensions of Northeast Asian energy cooperation, especially among Russia, China and Japan, that have driven significant investment, production and trade actions on a project basis and in specific locations of strategic value for regionalism, without triggering formal institutionalization. Consistent with Edward Luttwak's global observation in 1990s that economic measures taken by state and nonstate actors will increasingly become the preferred means of statecraft, we observe that the supplier and consumer relations in the NEA LNG market have generated tangible impact on capital allocation, physical connectivity through transport infrastructure development, and network dynamics that have major effects on regional players' security and commercial interests and their willingness to engage in confidence-building measures and cooperative games under political pressures and market shocks.[22] Chatham House's leading Eurasian energy politics expert, Keun-Wook Paik, has noted that these games have gained greater value in the post-unipolar moment, as the United States and Russia have seen a steady erosion of their influence over political economic outcomes—and arguably lost their self-restraint from disruptive unilateralism—prompting emerging and secondary powers to find new means of risk management to achieve national energy security.[23] Therefore we move beyond the international political economy literature's primary focus on system level analysis of how globalization impacts policymaking and energy decision-making, toward analysis of underlying political and market forces shaping power plays and mechanics of inter-state energy relations.[24] Our empirical story below shows how a geoeconomic process of integration-by-regionalization, via the instrumentalization of collaborative gas pipeline projects

---

[19] Yun and Zhang (2006).
[20] Choo (2016) p. 95.
[21] Ibid, pp. 100–103.
[22] Luttwak (1990).
[23] Paik (2012).
[24] Blackwill and Harris (2016).

and inter-state LNG networks, may well lead to newer dynamics of energy security and economic order— that may under favourable conditions transcend the barriers to regionalism mentioned above, which are largely legacies of historical animosities, "high" politics and "hard" security arrangements of post-WWII U.S. unipolarity in NEA.

Rising LNG Demand from NEA Economies and National Responses

The most significant market and domestic energy policy trend common to Northeast Asian countries in the first two decades of the twenty-first century is the energy transition through natural gas toward renewables. This trend is consistent with the rising global natural gas demand, which was forecast by IEA (2019) to increase by 1.7 times from 3,505 bcm to 5,986 bcm from 2016–50, of which non-OECD (Organisation for Economic Cooperation and Development) countries will account for 87 percent of the increase.[25] Natural gas consumption is forecast to grow by 2.7 times in Asia from 2016 to 2050, bringing the region's share in the total global consumption from 19 to 29 percent. Given the lack of domestic sources in Japan and South Korea and the underdevelopment of a regional pipeline network, LNG has become the critical medium for the transition. Again, NEA dovetails global trends— IEA (2019) projects that by year 2030, the global demand for LNG will increase to 4.7 trillion cubic meters, and to 5.7 tcm in 2050.[26] Developing economies in Asia have been a powerful engine for this LNG thirst, with their market share of LNG in total gas demand projected to grow from 20% in 2018 to 40% by 2040.[27] For this demand, Asian countries have paid a "premium" which has been sticky since the Fukushima nuclear accident. Between 2010 and 2013, Asian LNG prices for NEA rose from $10–12 per mmbtu (million British thermal units) to $15–18 per mmbtu. Low Henry Hub prices combined with soaring LNG prices in Asia have generated considerable interest among Asian buyers to acquire cheaper gas and explore alternatives to the current pricing structures, which is not market clearing but linked to crude oil import prices.[28] This section briefly surveys these trends and discusses implications for energy cooperation and market governance frameworks in NEA.

A. Japan

Japanese energy security regarding natural gas has been shaped by both domestic demand side management measures, as well as geopolitical opportunities under President Trump's energy policy and foreign economic statecraft. Energy usage in Japan

---

[25] Itoh (2021).

[26] https://thebarentsobserver.com/en/arctic-lng/2021/03/push-global-lead-lng-moscow-takes-aim-arctic-tundra

[27] IEA (2019).

[28] IEA (2020).

remains highly dependent on fossil fuels, as domestic energy production covered only 12% of total energy supply in 2019.[29] Energy production has decreased (significantly due to the Fukushima disaster 2011) by 32.44% since 1990. This is all whilst electricity consumption has increased 22.03% from 1990.[30] World Economic Outlook (2018) forecasted Japan's natural gas demand to decrease by 0.7 percent per annum from 2017 to 2040 due to the restart of its nuclear reactors and ongoing improvements in energy efficiency and utilization of renewable sources.[31]

Nonetheless, as one of the largest LNG importers, the security of gas supply is a major and long-term concern for Japan. A shortage of gas supply for the power sector in January 2021 resulted in purchases of spot cargos at record high prices—higher than prices after the 2011 Fukushima disaster. Already by 2018, the total cost of Japan's LNG imports had risen to approximately 2.3 times that of 2010.[32] Policy responses have focused on increasing the share of gas imports developed by Japanese companies—what the Ministry of Economy, Trade and Industry (METI) calls the "independent development ratio." METI aims to raise the ratio to 40% for oil and natural gas, and to 60% for coal by 2030.[33] The Japanese government has also encouraged the diversification of LNG supply, launching in 2021 the first LNG transport from Australia.[34] In 2019, over one-third (39%) of imports came from Australia, followed by Malaysia (13%), Qatar (11%), the Russian Federation (8%) and Brunei (6%).[35] Naturally, Russian supply is of intense interest as it would avoid the "Asian premium." Russia has signalled its interest in providing to Japan—in June 2018, Russian Deputy Energy Minister Pavel Sorokin said that Russia might increase its LNG production up to 100 or 120 mt/y by 2035. As U.S. President Donald Trump reached out to Asia from a position of strength in terms of historical domestic energy production and a sharp ideological and security pivot to Asia to stem Chinese threats, Japan has found itself in a delicate political situation. The Japan-U.S. Strategic Partnership was established in November 2017 with the aim of developing new LNG markets globally, but with Biden's reduction of American fossil fuel production, it remains to be seen what potential there might be to address Japan's needs.[36] IEA (2021a, b) notes that "Tokyo's strategy of politicising energy to capture Moscow's attention, thereby improving bilateral relations, if somewhat ignorant of economic rationality, may negatively affect marketing opportunities for

---

[29] IEA (2021a, b).

[30] https://www.iea.org/countries/japan.

[31] Itoh (2021).

[32] Ibid, p. 26.

[33] IEA (2021a, b) *Japan 2021*, Ibid, p. 30.

[34] https://www.spglobal.com/commodityinsights/en/market-insights/latest-news/electric-power/122320-commodities-2021-japan-to-enter-new-era-of-hydrogen-in-2021-with-launch-of-liquefied-transport.

[35] Ibid, p.161.

[36] Ibid, p. 29.

US LNG suppliers."[37] One could add to this equation Russia's pariah status after the invasion of Ukraine in spring of 2022.

Given the fluctuating geopolitical pressures, Japan has sought stability in domestic regulatory reform approaches to address energy security, market-based instruments such as credit trading, carbon tax and carbon border adjustments to cost-effectively reduce emissions and foster domestic firms' adaptation and innovation.[38] The national goal to achieve carbon-neutrality by 2050 will accelerate the deployment of low-carbon technologies and redress regulatory and institutional barriers.[39] The Green Growth Strategy aims to raise renewables to between 50–60% of electricity demand in 2050, with 10% from hydrogen and ammonia generation.[40] There is a push from the industry and epistemic community for hydrogen energy.[41] As METI talked about a "hydrogen-based society," Japan aims to have 800 000 fuel cell vehicles, more than 5 million residential fuel cells, and to establish an international hydrogen-ammonia supply chain by 2030.[42]

METI has also shown vested interest in the concept of a transregional energy platform. It has advocated the development of "an internationally accepted LNG trading hub" to pull in LNG trade from around the world and to establish a universal price discovery mechanism by increasing spot trading to enhance the reliability of spot price indices, which could result in the elimination of the Asian premium.[43] This platform will be mutually supportive of an open power supply infrastructure by allowing third party access, such as policies to liberalize electricity and gas markets, coordinate firms, and monitor prices, starting at home. Japan established the Organization for Cross-regional Coordination of Transmission Operators in 2015 to "balance electricity supply and demand on a nationwide level and to improve power interchange across regions."[44] It set up the Electricity and Gas Market Surveillance Commission (EGC) in 2016 to monitor the market and promote competition.

Japan has also put up resources for basic research in support of energy transition and efficiency goals. Public investment is high for international standards, with the government energy Research & Development (R&D) spending reaching 314 billion

---

[37] Ibid, p. 30.

[38] https://www.iea.org/countries/japan.

[39] IEA (2021a, b).

[40] Ibid, p. 14.

[41] A leading energy expert, Nobuo Tanaka of Tanaka Global, has made a strong case for it to in numerous public forums. https://plus.iru-miru.com/en/article/38916; http://worldfuturefuelsummit.in/downloads/PPT/PS-5/Nobuo_TANAKA_Hydrogen.pdf; https://www.asia-hydrogen-summit.com/speakers/nobuo-tanaka/.

[42] Ibid p. 14; METI (2017), Basic Hydrogen Strategy, METI, Tokyo, www.meti.go.jp/english/press/2017/pdf/1226_003b.pdf, p. 5. The athletes' village for the Tokyo Summer Olympic 2021 was the world's first hydrogen-powered town. https://www.ammoniaenergy.org/articles/japans-road-map-for-fuel-ammonia/; https://www.world-energy.org/article/19439.html.

[43] METI (2016) Strategy for LNG Market Development: Creating Flexible LNG Market and Developing an LNG Trading Hub in Japan, METI, Tokyo, www.meti.go.jp/english/press/2016/pdf/0502_01b.pdf, p. 6.

[44] IEA (2021a, b) *Japan 2021*, IEA, Paris, https://www.iea.org/reports/japan-2021, p. 29.

yen (USD 2.88 billion) in 2018.[45] In 2021, Japan announced plans to mobilize 30 trillion yen (USD 275 billion) of public and private investment for R&D on the environment and energy in the next decade.[46] However, with any push in public policy, the Japanese government faces criticisms of the displacement of private efforts and stunting market development, leading METI to reiterate a "private first" approach.[47]

B. South Korea

As with Japan, oil constitutes the largest energy source for ROK, making up 39% of Total Primary Energy Supply (TPES) in 2018 and 52% of Total Final Consumption (TFC) in 2018, with coal as the second-largest energy source in TPES, accounting for 29% in 2018.[48] Natural gas demand has grown in recent decades, accounting for 17% of TPES in 2018.[49] Even more reliant on imported fossil fuel, Korean domestic production covered only around 1% of total demand, creating an intense sense of insecurity.[50] The ROK government continues to work out its vision for a sustainable energy transition, with demand management goals to improve energy intensity by 38% over the 2017 level and reduce energy demand by 18.6% compared by 2040.[51] The Green New Deal of 2020 talked of building smart grids and promoting green vehicles such as hydrogen and electric, with goals to distribute 200,000 hydrogen passenger cars, buses and trucks, install 450 refuelling stations, and expand hydrogen distribution infrastructure such as production facilities.[52]

As with Japan, Korea has no significant inter-country electricity and gas connections. The ROK government has expressed a "commitment to the creation of a North East Asia Super Grid, to enhance not only energy security, but also the competitiveness of Korea's domestic renewable energy industry."[53] As with its Japanese counterpart, it offers domestic regulatory incentives while pursuing diversification of imports. In April 2019, ROK lowered the tax burden on LNG, while raising it on bituminous coal.[54] In 2018, Qatar accounted for 32% of total imports, followed by Australia (18%), the United States (11%), Oman (10%), Malaysia (8%), Indonesia (8%) and the Russian Federation (4%).[55] ROK became the largest importer of U.S. LNG in 2018, and the state-owned Korea Gas Corporation (KOGAS) signed an agreement with BP in 2019 to buy 1.58 million tonnes (mt) of U.S. LNG for 15 years

---

[45] Ibid, p. 111.

[46] Ibid.

[47] METI (2016) Strategy for LNG Market Development: Creating Flexible LNG Market and Developing an LNG Trading Hub in Japan, METI, Tokyo, www.meti.go.jp/english/press/2016/pdf/0502_01b.pdf, p. 9.

[48] IEA (2020) Korea 2020, IEA, Paris, https://www.iea.org/reports/korea-2020, p. 17.

[49] Ibid, p. 18.

[50] Ibid, p. 20.

[51] Ibid, p. 22.

[52] Ibid, p. 26.

[53] IEA (2020) "Korea 2020 Energy Policy Review," p. 2.

[54] Ibid, p. 126.

[55] Ibid, p. 142.

starting in 2025. KOGAS purchases most of its LNG through long-term supply contracts and uses spot cargos to correct small market imbalances.[56] Currently KOGAS operates five major LNG terminals, and South Korea also has reloading capabilities to re-export LNG at the POSCO and K-Power jointly owned Gwangyang regasification facility and terminal.[57] Due to KOGAS's monopoly on gas supply and high LNG resale prices at home, private firms are incentivized to invest in regasification capacity and purchase LNG on the global market.[58]

Regionally, ROK has discussed cooperation with China and Japan to improve the transparency and flexibility of the global LNG market.[59] However, as noted, the regional forums have not led to concrete collaborative actions. Technical solutions such as the digitalization of the energy supply chain and the overall energy system have been proposed, but it is not clear how they could reduce national energy security and address emerging threats.[60] More directly impactful are early efforts at cross-border interconnections, with KOGAS and Russian Gazprom signing a Memorandum of Understanding (MoU) in 2008 to investigate the construction of a 1200 km pipeline via the Democratic People's Republic of Korea (DPRK) to supply Russian gas to South Korea. This effort was suspended in 2013 but renewed in 2018, and the two state-controlled firms are currently conducting a joint study on the possibility of a pipeline project.[61]

C. China

Electricity generation in China is still largely provided by coal-burning at 66% of electricity produced in 2018, followed by hydropower (17%), wind (4%), nuclear (4%), natural gas (3%), and solar (2.5%).[62] While renewable sources have garnered massive investments and high hopes for China's energy transition, various political-institutional factors have greatly curtailed the renewable energy usage in the domestic grid, leaving natural gas in its critical role as a transition fuel.[63] PRC's demand for natural gas is projected to expand by 2.8 times from 2016 to 2040, when China will account for approximately 20 percent of the global gas consumption.[64] It is also projected to account for one-third of the total growth in the global LNG trade from 2018 to 2024, overtaking Japan as the largest LNG importer at 109 bcm (or about 80 mt) by 2024.[65] To this end, China has begun to develop LNG transportation infrastructure at home, with nearly 30,000 LNG fuelled trucks and 25 mill tonnes

---

[56] Ibid.
[57] https://www.iea.org/articles/korea-natural-gas-security-policy.
[58] Ibid.
[59] Ibid, p. 27.
[60] Ibid, p. 30.
[61] Ibid, p. 148.
[62] IEA (2021a, b) *The Role of China's ETS in Power Sector Decarbonisation*, IEA, Paris, https://www.iea.org/reports/the-role-of-chinas-ets-in-power-sector-decarbonisation, p. 25.
[63] Lin and Purra (2019), https://ideas.repec.org/a/eee/enepol/v124y2019icp401-410.html.
[64] IEA (2021a, b) *The Role of China's ETS in Power Sector Decarbonisation*, p. 25.
[65] Ibid, p. 22.

of small-scale LNG delivered (accounting for 50% of China's LNG demand) in 2018.[66] As a result of the ongoing Sino-American trade war, U.S. supplies of LNG to China was cancelled. Australian gas and coal export to China has met with a similar political fate. Consequently, Russia should be moving up from its status as China's third largest gas supplier in 2021.[67] With a predicted shortfall of 270 bcm by 2030, China is likely to turn up the delivery from Russia's Power of Siberia (PoS) pipeline project and the "D" line from Turkmenistan into western China. Further gas supply is already manifesting itself in the form of Novatek LNG's Yamal and ALNG2 projects, and in the later 2020s, Novatek ALNG's 1 and 3.[68] All these LNG projects include Chinese financing, equity participation (upstream and midstream), and/or with Belt and Road Initiative (BRI) involvement—or all three! In the foreseeable future, China will likely overtake Japan as the world's biggest consumer of LNG, and become entrenched in Russian LNG supplies. Hence it will gain price setting leverage in negotiations with LNG suppliers including Australia, Russia, Qatar, and the U.S. If the PRC were to take a lead in forming a NEA LNG market/hub, it would likely have a major say in its pricing and trading parameters.

Lastly, and applied generally to NEA countries, recent transport infrastructure developments, notably the rapid ascendency of Northeast Asian countries as global shipping powers, the intensification of intra-Asian shipping networks centered increasingly on Chinese ports, and the historic expansion of the Panama Canal in 2017 which enables large LNG ships to pass expediently from North America to Asia, have created major and complex effects on energy markets and politics in Asia.[69] Under Trump's presidency, Japan, ROK and Taiwan increased their purchase of American LNG, whereas China dropped its interest in the face of escalating trade war and security conflicts.

A Future Sub-Regional Monopoly in Gas Supply in the Making?

In international relations theories, a hegemon could push for regime-building that provides common goods and system stability. Historically, as Eurasia's largest fossil fuel producer and holder of deposits, Russia has conducted a set of balancing acts to translate its supplier status to geopolitical advantages, which remained largely un-institutionalized by design. Instead, Russia and its consumer partners have been relying on the inherent nature of energy infrastructure such as pipelines and terminals

---

[66] IEA (2019) *World Energy Outlook 2019*, IEA, Paris, https://www.iea.org/reports/world-energy-outlook-2019, p. 206.
[67] https://www.energypolicy.columbia.edu/research/qa/qa-china-russia-energy-relations-will-new-oil-and-natural-gas-deals-help-russia-weather-economic.
[68] Reilly (2021).
[69] Lin (2019).

to underpin bilateral geoeconomic relations, as these projects and contracts are long-term in financial, economic and political impact, and the number of government and private players are few and often locked into long-term relations.[70] Given the lack of institutionalization in NEA cooperation across a range of issues, Russia's strategy as a politics-first oil exporter would seem to reinforce this tendency for a lack of cross-border coordinated government-market relations beyond those captured in bilateral economic strategic agreements. However, this expectation should not be a given, for there are fundamental technological, developmental, and environmental trends that could create a firmer basis for mutual confidence and perceived necessity in multilateral cooperation. Alternatively, disruptive technologies such as blue/green hydrogen and market swings could pre-empt extant political resistance to a regional approach to energy security.

Predictions prior to 2022 had Russia accounting for 12 percent of the gas production growth in the world from 2017–40.[71] It holds technically recoverable natural gas reserves of 49.3 trillion cubic meters—20% of the world's total—of which a significant portion is under the ice and water of the Russian Arctic.[72] What Russia could hope to gain economically from this resource base is highly dependent on preconditions for infrastructure development, financial provisions, and governing institutions.[73] Russia has stable strategic goals on structural diversification towards LNG and non-carbon exports, digital transformation and institutionalization of energy industries, more equitable spatial distribution of energy infrastructure with a prioritization of Eastern Siberia, Far East and Arctic regions, and promotion of low-carbon development due to climate change.[74] At the same time, Russia is highly dependent on external finance, multinational corporations' technologies in exploration and production, and environmental risk management, as well as sustained European and Asian demand to realize its geopolitical leverage. In the early 2000s during the height of global stature of BRICS and the nadir of Western liberal regime-building, signalled by the impasse over the Doha Round of WTO negotiation, Russia had sought energy cooperation with fellow BRICS members. However, a general decline of the developmental fortunes of non-Chinese BRICS countries and self-inflicted geopolitical shocks in 2014 and 2022 have severely reduced options for Russia, leading to greater reliance on NEA countries' cooperation—in particular on China as the primary energy consumer, provider of finance and technology, and reliable security partner.[75]

However, most recently in 2023, Russia has invited countries such as Turkey, Saudi Arabia, and India to consider equity investment and/or project participation in Russia's flagship LNG operation on the Yamal Peninsula, Novatek LNG, to replace

---

[70] Nordstream is a classic example. Reilly (2021) p. 49.

[71] IEA (2021a, b) *Japan 2021*, IEA, Paris, https://www.iea.org/reports/japan-2021, p. 21.

[72] Ibid p. 47.

[73] Reilly (2021).

[74] https://eng.brics-russia2020.ru/images/114/89/1148985.pdf, p. 38.

[75] Henderson and Moe (2019).

the Western consortia which have largely withdrawn under the US and EU sanctions.[76] This move's timing is in broad alignment with growing Sino-Russian discussions about the possible expansion of the BRICS membership, to include states such as Saudia Arabia, Iran, Turkey, Algeria and Argentina, and possibly later additional (gas-rich) countries like Kazakhstan, Nigeria and Egypt.[77] This may reflect early signs of the formation of a BRICS-backed, gas-equivalent of OPEC, centered around the NEA gas and LNG markets.

Nonetheless, at this stage Novatek's emphasis is very much on developing major new LNG markets, for instance in India. But crucially, China still remains in the Novatek Consortia, is now agreeing to the development of the Power of Siberia 3 project (via Mongolia), and is building three of the turbines for Arctic LNG2, thus showing no sign of withdrawing from this Novatek flagship venture with Russia in the Arctic.[78] It is reasonable to suggest that Beijing may be positioning itself as both the dominant consumer and a significant partner to Russia in supplying an augmented LNG trading hub in NEA served by emerging gas upstream and midstream consortiums. In this advantageous position, China could capture benefits from the extended LNG global value chain, at the same time bolster its energy security needs.[79]

A. Long-term Russian interest in a preeminent regional supplier status

Russian President Putin's "pivot" to Asia statements in 2014 coincided with Moscow's decision that the Arctic would be the critical region for economic development/investment in the twenty-first century.[80] The key vehicle for monetizing an Arctic economy was the development of Novatek LNG's operation on the Arctic's Yamal Peninsula. It was imagined that this vehicle would attract Western technology, management know-how, proprietary knowledge (LNG systems and licences), and international investors and customers alike. It also furthered Putin's Arctic decree by maximizing the economic use of the Eurasia-spanning NSR, to channel LNG to clients in both Europe and Asia. For Russia, the strategic significance of the Arctic LNG gameplay is threefold: (1) geoeconomic leverage over NEA's power-generation capacity; (2) the use of the NSR as a major new maritime sea lines of communication to anchor Putin's Greater Eurasian Partnership vision, and concomitantly making credible the emergence of Russia as a Sea Power in NEA; and (3) the establishment of a new, digitally connected, regional LNG trading hub in NEA that Russia could substantially supply at a super-competitive price, and thereby reduce

---

[76] https://www.rivieramm.com/news-content-hub/news-content-hub/total-withdraws-directors-to-novatek-writes-down-us37bn-74240.

[77] https://www.silkroadbriefing.com/news/2022/11/09/the-new-candidate-countries-for-brics-expansion/.

[78] https://www.nasdaq.com/articles/russias-arctic-lng-2-will-use-chinese-equipment-for-power-generation-novatek.

[79] Zeng et al. (2022); China's strengthened—even in relative terms-market position could adversely affect Japan's: https://asia.nikkei.com/Business/Energy/China-tightens-grip-as-dominant-LNG-buyer-with-long-term-deals.

[80] Henderson and Moe (2019).

US/Western LNG industry competition and its potential geoeconomic influence in and over NEA.[81] It is not coincidental that these three factors coincide with China's energy and security interests, from both a geoeconomic and strategic point of view.

In this scheme of regional energy dominance, Moscow bets both on pipelines and maritime LNG transport routes. Given China's increasing number of pipeline deals with Central Asian countries, as well as the long-term cost implications of pipeline projects—notably the $400 billion gas deal signed in 2014, which has locked in Beijing to pay prices well above market prices in recent years—and potential inadequacy of Western Siberian deposits, both Russia and China have incentives to develop Russian LNG resources and routes.[82] The significance of pipeline delivery in bilateral geopolitical calculus became salient once more when, two weeks before the launch of Russian invasion of Ukraine in February 2022, Putin signed a new 30-year contract for Gazprom to supply gas to China National Petroleum Corp. (CNPC) via a new pipeline in the Russian Far East.[83]

In contrast to pipelines, LNG is evidently the market instrument for geoeconomic strategies. Given its technological and transport capacity for flexible delivery destination and multi-sourcing potentials, as well as the more discrete stages of the global LNG value-chain, the LNG industry provides far greater opportunities for transnational cooperation for government and private actors.[84] Even in the midst of Western sanctions of post-Crimea Russia, Novatek's LNG's Arctic projects continued to forge investment and production partnerships with French, Chinese, Japanese and Indian energy firms, and have been instrumental in these stakeholders' imagining of a potential regional, cooperative energy trading hub.[85] Right off the bat, China underwrote the projects' first output—Yamal LNG—by taking a direct equity-based position and offering financial support in face of financial sanctions imposed on the project by the West since 2014. Joining Gazprom and Rosneft in the two Sakhalin gas projects, Novatek further develops its relationship with Japanese, Chinese and European partners drawing together geographical resources of the Northern Sea Route, Russian Far East, and Russian Arctic.[86] Prior to the Russo-Ukraine war in 2022, Northeast Asia's burgeoning LNG market had been pursued by the biggest global suppliers—U.S., Australia, Qatar, and Russia—with the latter exerting a geographical

---

[81] Razmanova (2020).

[82] https://www.washingtonpost.com/world/europe/china-russia-sign-400-billion-gas-deal/2014/05/21/364e9e74-e0de-11e3-8dcc-d6b7fede081a_story.html.

[83] Notably, with the deal settled in euros. https://www.reuters.com/world/asia-pacific/exclusive-russia-china-agree-30-year-gas-deal-using-new-pipeline-source-2022-02-04/.

[84] The LNG value chain encompasses production, processing, and conversion of.
   natural gas to LNG, its long-distance transportation, and regasification. https://www.energy.gov/sites/default/files/2020/10/f79/LNG%20Value%20Chain%20Fact%20Sheet_1.pdf.

[85] Henderson and Yermakov (2019). Also see, https://www.highnorthnews.com/en/novatek-ships-yamal-lng-japan-uncertain-if-delivery-was-made-arctic; https://phys.org/news/2019-09-russia-novatek-huge-arctic-gas.html; https://jpt.spe.org/russian-lng-aims-high-leveraging-big-reserves-and-logistical-advantages.

[86] https://www.reuters.com/article/russia-rosneft-lng-idUKL5N25W2OI; https://www.novatek.ru/en/press/releases/index.php?id_4=4503.

advantage in promoting a *regional* energy approach with the Asian consumers—i.e. "regionalization-by-gasification". It had seemed like critical pieces were falling in place for a LNG-centered framework for regional integration in energy market and policies, led by quasi-private actors backed by geoeconomic statecraft.[87]

B. Chinese and Japanese stakes in private sector Russian gas projects

Established in 1994 and led by Putin's close ally, Leonid Mikhelson, Novatek serves as a new vehicle for regional gas supplies and scarce private sector partnerships. It holds a 50.1% stake in Yamal LNG; while France's Total holds 20%, China's CNPC holds 20% and PRC's Silk Road Fund 9.9%.[88] Starting in 2020, Novatek has shipped LNG from the Yamal project to Japan eastbound via the Northern Sea Route.[89] The success of the first Yamal project led to plans for developing a second LNG terminal planned to commence 2023—a 19.8 million mt/year, Arctic LNG 2 project—with Chinese and Japanese shareholders. Novatek has a 60% stake in Arctic LNG 2.[90] Chinese national oil companies CNPC and China National Offshore Oil Corp. each holds a 10% stake.[91] A consortium (Japan Arctic LNG) of Mitsui and the government-owned Japan Oil, Gas and Metals National Corporation holds a 10% stake in the Arctic LNG 2 project.[92] Close to home, Japanese firms have invested in the Sakhalin gas fields in the RFE. Mitsui and Mitsubishi hold 12.5% and 10% stakes respectively in the Sakhalin-2 gas project. By 2022, 60% of LNG output from Sakhalin-2 had gone to Japan, constituting around 10% of Japan's total LNG import.[93] Under pressure from Western firms' exit after Russia's invasion of Ukraine in 2022, Japanese Prime Minister Kishida has reiterated his government's commitment to Sakhalin-2.[94] The estimated cost of replacing Sakhalin gas with spot market supplies would be $15 billion, which would raise the cost of Japanese import of LNG by one-third per year.[95]

There are further plans to develop a conventional onshore gas field located on the Gydan Peninsula within the Arctic Circle, in the north of the Russian Federation, and

---

[87] See Reilly (2021) on "polycentric regionalism".

[88] https://www.spglobal.com/platts/en/market-insights/latest-news/natural-gas/072420-russias-novatek-ships-first-lng-cargo-to-japan-eastbound-via-northern-sea-route.

[89] https://www.spglobal.com/platts/en/market-insights/latest-news/natural-gas/072420-russias-novatek-ships-first-lng-cargo-to-japan-eastbound-via-northern-sea-route.

[90] Ibid.

[91] https://seanews.ru/en/2019/08/01/en-mitsubishi-not-investing-in-arctic-lng-2/.

[92] http://www.gasprocessingnews.com/news/mitsui,-jogmec-to-invest-in-novateks-arctic-lng-2-project.aspx.

[93] https://asia.nikkei.com/Business/Energy/No-easy-exit-for-Japan-from-Russia-S-Sakhalin-2-LNG-project. If the Japanese firms had exited following Shell, there would've been no guarantee that Japan would continue to receive any LNG from Sakhalin.

[94] https://www.reuters.com/world/asia-pacific/japan-will-not-abandon-sakhalin-2-lng-stake-kishida-says-2022-03-31/; https://asia.nikkei.com/Business/Energy/Japan-backed-Sakhalin-2-LNG-project-rocked-by-Shell-exit.

[95] https://asia.nikkei.com/Business/Energy/Replacing-Russian-LNG-from-Sakhalin-2-would-cost-Japan-15bn.

to construct natural gas and liquefaction facilities.[96] Beyond LNG, Novatek has also been in talks with Mitsui over an ammonia project in the Arctic, expected to start 2026, which would convert renewable electricity into an energy-rich gas that can easily be cooled and stored in a liquid fuel cells to power vehicles.[97] Consistent with this possibility, Mitsui O.S.K. Lines re-entered the ammonia transport space with the charter of the ammonia and LNG carrier *Green Pioneer*.[98] South Korea, which has been absent in these energy investment projects, is expected to capitalize on this new energy source development. Shipbuilding & Offshore Engineering (KSOE) will develop ammonia-fuelled ships for certification by Korean Register (KR), while Lotte Global Logistics and Hyundai Merchant Marine will operate those ships.[99] Japanese and South Korean shipbuilding (LNG vessels and icebreakers) represents midstream investment in Novatek's LNG operation by its regional customers, further fleshing out these players' niches and commitments to a regional LNG value chain.

In sum, the above commercial tie-ups have robust and enduring values in national energy security terms.[100] Tim Reilly has demonstrated that "the forming up of an LNG networked institutional structure (equity holders, operators, service providers and financing instruments such as the Silk Road Fund) under the banner of the Novatek partnership, constitutes a fledgling *institutional component* of industrial P-R in NEA."[101] As Russia's leading private energy firm, Novatek receives subsidies from the Russian government and benefits from industrial policies for domestic manufacturing, including tax incentives and promotion of commercial technologies at home and abroad.[102]

---

[96] Ibid.

[97] https://www.reuters.com/business/energy/russias-novatek-talks-with-japans-mitsui-ammonia-project-kommersant-says-2021-06-24/; https://lngprime.com/other-fuels/novatek-in-ammonia-talks-with-mitsui/23292/.

[98] https://www.mol.co.jp/en/pr/2021/21042.html.

[99] https://www.ammoniaenergy.org/articles/the-ammonia-wrap-two-new-large-scale-ammonia-projects-in-the-uae-and-more/.

[100] Quoting Mitsui, "abundant natural gas reserves and geographical superiority in terms of access to major LNG demand areas, we will contribute to the stable supply of energy to the world, including Japan." https://www.mitsui.com/jp/en/release/2019/1229585_11219.html.

[101] Reilly (2021), p. 22.

[102] Tim Reilly, "A Sino-Russian LNG Venture in the Eurasian Arctic," p. 13.

Conclusion: Turning Geoeconomics on Its Head? Implications of Russia's Invasion of Ukraine 2022

The short- to medium-term effect of Western economic pressures on Russia is to drive Russia further into Beijing's arms.[103] President Putin's visit of Beijing in December 2021 and the range of agreements signed on energy, food, and finance reflected a mutual effort to consolidate the geoeconomic relationship to brace for the onslaught of Western responses to the Russian invasion of Ukraine. The Chinese Coast Guard—Russian Federal Security Service Memorandum of Understanding, signed in Murmansk in May 2023, is directly linked to the sovereignty and enforcement of Russia's Northern Sea Route (NSR). This move has significant implications as this new global Sea Line of Communication (SLOC), links northern Eurasia from the Barents Sea in Europe to the Bering Strait in NE Asia, and facilitates the movement of Russian Arctic LNG to markets spanning Eurasia. In spite of sanctions, Arctic projects like Novatek LNG are increasingly competitive on pricing, volumes, and availability/access, benefitting China (and other countries such as India) in terms of the security of energy supply. This Sino-Russian MoU is also significant as a precursor to Russia and China becoming regional blue-water maritime powers in the NSR's Eurasian Arctic.

In the short-term, Japan and ROK would be restrained from accepting Russian energy.[104] What remains unclear is whether Russia's increased isolation and energy cooperation with China will reduce or increase the need for regional cooperation in NEA. In other words, would Russia's closer peg to China's oil and gas demands reduce or increase the momentum for the formation of a regional energy market? Might Russia's cooperation with China fuel competitive dynamics among neighboring countries?[105] By exacerbating South Korea's and Japan's energy security concerns, might Russia incentivize these countries to focus on bilateral relations and extra-regional energy relations (with U.S., Australia, Southeast Asia, the Middle East, etc.), instead of regional cooperation in NEA? Is Russian's long-term geostrategy to strike a strategic balance between European and Asian demands for its oil and gas in Eurasia, and between China and Japanese and Korean demands in the regional sense, effectively defunct for the foreseeable future? What other energy relations, such as with India and Central Asian countries, might Moscow put in place to adapt to a gloomy outlook of worsening asymmetry vis-à-vis Beijing?

---

[103] https://www.csis.org/analysis/can-russia-execute-gas-pivot-asia; https://www.rivieramm.com/news-content-hub/news-content-hub/exxonmobil-leaving-russia-sakhalin-1-70040.

[104] https://www.bloomberg.com/news/videos/2022-03-28/japan-ahead-tanaka-global-ceo-nobuo-tanaka-video.

[105] Japan is concerned that Chinese takeover of Shell shares after the latter's exit amidst sanctions on Russia in 2022 would increase the chance of a Sino-Russian consensus to downgrade provisions for Japan. https://theprint.in/world/japan-concerned-over-china-russia-lng-alliance-after-shell-exits-sakhalin-2/928008/; https://www.offshore-technology.com/news/chinese-shells-russian-gas/.

In the second half of 2022 and first half of 2023, the PRC appears to be leveraging two geopolitical factors to diversify its oil relations with Middle East producers—first, the Biden Administration's uneasy relations with the Saudi Crown Prince Mohammed bin Salman. This is suggested in the recent announcement of Saudi Aramco building a major refining complex in NE China and further investing in a multi-billion joint venture petrochemical facility.[106] The second leverage for China is the impasse in bilateral and multilateral negotiations over nuclear agreements and changes in sanctions on Iran.[107] The culmination of Beijing's opportunism was the Chinese brokered meetings between Iran and Saudi Arabia in early 2023, which stoked discussions by Arab producers on trading LNG in the Chinese currency (RMB).[108] While these transactions are far from projecting a rosy future for RMB internationalization, they clearly indicate the tightening relations between Russia, the Middle East and Iran, and China as mutually beneficial responses to geopolitical pressures applied by the US. These unfolding effects should be examined as a *geoeconomic* consequence of the Biden Administration's clear prioritization of the Indo-Pacific and European theatres, and not as unrelated or inevitable trade-off of America's ongoing conflicts with Russia, Iran and China. The Chinese Coast Guard—FSB MoU, however, is the first unambiguous sign of the intensification of Sino-Russian energy-related relations leading to a bilateral regional governance framework, despite and perhaps even because of the East–West nature of events in Ukraine.

References

Aggarwal and Lin. (2001). APEC as an Institution. In Richard E. Feinberg & Ye Zhao (Eds.), *Assessing APEC's Progress: Trade, Ecotech, and Institutions*, Singapore ISEAS.
Basu, M. (2019, 2 Sept). *Inside SoftBank CEO's vision for an Asian supergrid*. GovInsider Asia. https://govinsider.asia/intl-en/article/asia-super-grid-masayoshi-son-renewables-energy-institute-mika-ohbayashi-japan
Blackwill and Harris. (2016). *War by Other Means*. Harvard University Press.
Calder, K. (2005). *Korea's Energy Insecurities*. KEI, p. 4.
Choo, J. (2016). Energy cooperation problems in Northeast Asia: Unfolding the reality. *East Asia, 23*, 100.
Diesen, G. (2018). *Russia's geoeconomic strategy for a greater Eurasia*. Routledge.
Ding, T., et al. (2020). Joint electricity and carbon market for Northeast Asia energy interconnection. *Global Energy Interconnection, 3*(2), 99–110.
Freeman, C. (2015). Building an energy cooperation regime in Northeast Asia. In K. Bo, & J. Ku (Eds.) *Energy Security Cooperation in Northeast Asia*. Routledge.

---

[106] https://www.reuters.com/business/energy/saudi-aramco-open-new-china-refinery-petchem-complex-2026-2023-03-26/.

[107] https://www.bloomberg.com/news/newsletters/2023-04-22/china-is-slowly-moving-into-the-middle-east-new-economy-saturday.

[108] https://www.energyintel.com/00000186-3aad-d94d-a19e-bbedc2700004; https://www.al-monitor.com/originals/2023/03/china-settles-first-lng-trade-yuan-uae-deal.

Guy, C. K., Leung, Raymond Li, & Melissa Low. (2011). Transitions in China's oil economy, 1990–2010. *Eurasian Geography and Economics, 52/4,* 483–500.

Henderson, J., & Moe, A. (2019). *The Globalization of Russian Gas: Political and Commercial Catalysts.* Edward Elgar Publishing.

Henderson, J., & Yermakov, V. (2019, November). *Russian LNG: Becoming a Global Force.* Oxford Institute for Energy Studies, NG 154.

IEA. (2019). *World Energy Outlook 2019.* IEA, Paris, p. 175. https://www.iea.org/reports/world-energy-outlook-2019.

IEA. (2020). *Korea 2020.* IEA, Paris, p. 150. https://www.iea.org/reports/korea-2020.

IEA. (2021a). *Japan 2021a.* IEA, Paris, p. 22. https://www.iea.org/reports/japan-2021.

IEA. (2021b). *Japan 2021b.* IEA, Paris, p. 13. https://www.iea.org/reports/japan-2021.

Itoh, S. (2021). Energy outlook in the Asia-Pacific. *Russian Energy Strategy in the Asia-Pacific: Implications for Australia,* ANU Press, p. 18.

Korneev, K., Korneev, A. (2019). Institutions of international energy cooperation in North-East Asia region. *E3S Web of Conferences, 77,* 01004. Regional Energy Policy of Asian Russia 2018. https://doi.org/10.1051/e3sconf/20197701004

Lin, K.-C. (2019, March). Ports, shipping and grand strategy in the Indo-Pacific. In J. Hemmings (Ed.), *Infrastructure, ideas, and strategy in the Indo-Pacific* (Chapter 1). Henry Jackson Society Asia Studies Centre. https://henryjacksonsociety.org/wp-content/uploads/2019/04/HJS-Infrastructure-Ideas-and-Strategy-in-Indo-Pacific-web.pdf

Lin, K.-C., & Purra, M. M. (2019). Transforming China's electricity sector: Politics of institutional change and regulation. *Energy Policy, 124*(C), 401–410.

Luttwak, E. N. (1990). From geopolitics to geo-economics: Logic of conflict, grammar of Commerce. *The National Interest,* pp. 17–23.

Paik, K.-W. (2012). *Sino-Russian Oil and Gas Cooperation.* Oxford University Press/OIES.

Razmanova, Steblyanskaya. (2020). Arctic LNG cluster: New opportunities or new threats? *IOP Conference Series: Earth and Environmental Science,* IOP Publishing, 012165.

Reilly, T. (2021). Towards polycentric regionalism: Sino-Russian geo-economic relations and the formation of the Pacific Arctic Region. PhD thesis, University of Cambridge. https://api.repository.cam.ac.uk/server/api/core/bitstreams/58ec2a62-1f24-4595-94da-a46d2cf1db2d/content

Schultheiss, C. (2020). Joint development of hydrocarbon resources in the South China sea after the Philippines versus China arbitration? *Ocean Development & International Law, 51*(3), 241–262.

Schultheiss, C. (2021). Overcoming violence in maritime conflicts with provisional arrangements: A legal tool for conflict resolution. In M. Weller, M. Retter, & A. Varga (Eds.) *International Law and Peace Settlements,* pp. 525–544.

Thorarinsson, L. (2018, February). A review of the evolution of the Japanese oil industry, oil policy and its relationship with the Middle East. *OIES PAPER: WPM, 76,* 9.

Yun, W.-C., & Zhang, Z. X. (2005). Electric power grid interconnection in Northeast Asia. *Energy Policy, 34*(15), 2298–2309.

Zeng, W., et al. (2022). China's LNG import risk assessment based on the perspective of global governance. *Scientific Report, 12,* 15754. https://www.reuters.com/business/energy/2023-chinas-appetite-lng-set-rise-amid-tepid-demand-across-asia-2023-01-05/.

Open Access This chapter is licensed under the terms of the Creative Commons Attribution-NonCommercial-NoDerivatives 4.0 International License (http://creativecommons.org/licenses/by-nc-nd/4.0/), which permits any noncommercial use, sharing, distribution and reproduction in any medium or format, as long as you give appropriate credit to the original author(s) and the source, provide a link to the Creative Commons license and indicate if you modified the licensed material. You do not have permission under this license to share adapted material derived from this chapter or parts of it.

The images or other third party material in this chapter are included in the chapter's Creative Commons license, unless indicated otherwise in a credit line to the material. If material is not included in the chapter's Creative Commons license and your intended use is not permitted by statutory regulation or exceeds the permitted use, you will need to obtain permission directly from the copyright holder.

Chapter 11
The Liberal International Order and Economic Security

Kazuto Suzuki

Abstract The economic rise of China has made the country occupy a pivotal place in global supply chains, making Japan and the U.S. vulnerable to Chinese economic coercion in the form of sanctions and embargoes. Japan has created a new position of minister for economic security in the quest to reduce its dependence on China by diversifying supply sources for key materials and products, and augmenting stockpiles of strategic supplies. Such choices stem from the reality that China has joined the World Trade Organization (WTO) and enjoyed economic benefits from the free trade system, yet rejected its shared values and the rules of the liberal regime. The WTO mechanism is unable to identify and punish a member country's violation of the WTO rules, making it reasonable for Japan and the U.S. to strengthen their economic security and develop industrial policies in such a way that protects their industry. These steps should be understood as essentially protectionist; however, Japan intends to play its role as the leader of the free trade system and the rules-based international order by strictly limiting protections to "strategic" goods.

The Liberal Democratic Party's Recommendations on Economic Security

The idea of economic security that the Kishida administration highlights is based arguably on the Liberal Democratic Party's (LDP's) recommendations released in December 2020[1] and May 2021.[2] Those recommendations define economic security as ensuring "Japan's national interests … with economic measures." They propose to enhance Japan's "strategic autonomy" necessary for the country to protect its

---

[1] Liberal Democratic Party (2020).
[2] Liberal Democratic Party (2021).

K. Suzuki (✉)
Institute of Geoeconomics, International House of Japan, Tokyo, Japan

Graduate School of Public Policy, University of Tokyo, Tokyo, Japan

key industries and infrastructure from other countries' export bans, or supply chain disruptions, and to reinforce Japan's "strategic indispensability" to make the country integral to the global chain, thereby neutralizing efforts to disrupt trade with Japan. It is undeniable, however, that these recommendations look somewhat abstract.[3]

How much cost is the Kishida administration ready to incur to achieve "strategic autonomy" and to what extent will it make Japan's "strategic autonomy" compatible with free trade principles? Under the pretext of security, the Trump administration neglected free trade principles, imposing additional tariffs on steel and aluminum imports. The Biden administration follows suit. Yet, should Japan also downplay free trade principles?

The LDP recommendations focus principally on "defensive" measures, neglecting "offensive" ones. The enhancement of supply chain resilience and the reinforcement of critical infrastructures are proposed not only to protect the people's livelihoods and the national economy from economic pressures from foreign countries but also to avoid coming under economic pressures from other countries, thereby maintaining political independence as a nation. Undoubtedly, such "defensive" measures are significant, but these alone would be an economic "self-defense" and would not lead to a strategy of utilizing Japan's economic strength as power.

Japan's economic security promotion bill now in preparation also features this "defensive" stance. But there is another problem associated with such a stance: the government's increasing tendency to regulate corporate activities with penalties for technology leakage or the violation of relevant laws and regulations. Economic security means that the government has the authority to intervene in free business activities in the market. To this end, the government institutes penalties. Corporations, sensitive to such penalties, do not want to have their activities restrained due to increased compliance costs in order to comply with economic security promotion laws.

Supply Chain Imperatives

Among the measures in the economic security bill, high on the agenda are measures to boost the resilience of the supply chain. This is an issue that has received much attention of late, not only in Japan but around the world. U.S. President Joe Biden ordered a review of America's supply chains in February 2021,[4] and the European Parliament is deliberating measures to strengthen Europe's supply chain resilience.[5] A key factor driving these efforts is China's pivotal place in the global supply chains that have sprung up as a result of trade liberalization and market integration. The United States and China have become deeply interdependent economically, even as tensions have mounted over such flashpoints as China's authoritarian one-party

---

[3] Suzuki (2021).

[4] White House, Executive Order on America's Supply Chains (2021).

[5] European Parliament (2021).

rule, human rights violations, and military expansion. In the event that such tensions escalated into a serious clash, the United States and Japan would both be vulnerable to Chinese economic coercion in the form of sanctions and embargoes. Beijing has already demonstrated its willingness to use trade as a weapon against countries that provoke its ire, as seen in its ban on Taiwanese pineapple imports and its imposition of a wide range of punitive sanctions against Australia (including a ban on coal imports) after Prime Minister Scott Morrison called for a full-scale international investigation into the origins of the COVID-19 pandemic.[6]

With such security considerations in mind, policymakers have been looking at ways to reduce Japan's dependence on China, by, for example, diversifying our supply sources for key materials and products and augmenting our stockpiles of strategic supplies. It remains to be seen how the cabinet's economic security legislation will tackle these challenges, but the first step will doubtless be a thorough review of the nation's supply chains to assess our degree of dependence on Chinese suppliers.

Distinction Between Economic Security and Economic Statecraft

Alongside economic security with the three meanings mentioned above, there is another concept called "economic statecraft." Although economic security and economic statecraft are often confused, they should be distinguished from each other.

Economic statecraft means that a certain country "enforces upon other countries its own political will and values employing economic measures"—it overlaps with "economic coercion" in many ways with no distinct difference.[7] The condition for implementing economic statecraft is that a state has a "strategic indispensability" that gives it an advantage over other states. The state in question uses that advantage as leverage to enforce its political will and values on others. The "Global Magnitsky Act," which enforces standards of protecting human rights onto other countries, and economic sanctions against Iran and North Korea's nuclear development are both forms of economic statecraft.

In some cases, economic statecraft may be categorized as an "offensive" form of economic security. But fundamentally it should be considered to be different from economic security. A country uses economic statecraft to enforce upon a target country its political will and values by leveraging its economic superiority. The user of economic statecraft sets political objectives such as "improving the human rights situation in other countries" and uses its competitive industries and products as a means to achieve these goals. Once the country resorts to economic statecraft, trade with the target country will cease, resulting in economic losses. Other countries, fearing the possibility of future economic statecraft against them, will enhance their autonomy and reduce economic dependence or make their markets less open. This

---

[6] Wilson (2021).
[7] Blanchard and Ripsman (2008).

will damage the economic statecraft enforcer's international competitiveness and deprive it of business opportunities.

For example, the United States is restricting semiconductor transactions with China, calling on its allies to cooperate on semiconductor sanctions against China. The purpose of this move is to delay China's military and economic rise by making unavailable to the country semiconductors manufactured with advanced microfabrication technology while protecting technologies in which the United States and Western countries excel. As a result, however, semiconductor manufacturers cannot sell their most advanced semiconductors to the Chinese market, where demand for semiconductors rises. However, out of some consideration for the semiconductor business, semiconductors that are not cutting-edge products or are older generation products with wider line widths can be traded to China as general-purpose products.[8]

It should also be noted that economic statecraft is often described as "weaponization of interdependence,"[9] "weaponization of trade,"[10] or "war without weapons."[11] But its effects are different from those of military statecraft. As is manifest from sanctions against North Korea's nuclear and missile development, if economic statecraft fails to be effective on the target country—North Korea still pursues its nuclear development despite sanctions without changing its behavior—the enforcers of economic statecraft will lose much by the very act of launching economic statecraft. In preparation for the possible use of economic statecraft by others, any country must question its political readiness and evaluate the risk and how much damage may stem from economic statecraft.

Economic Security in the Free Trade Regime

Economic security has a marked "defensive" inclination and looks, therefore, like a protectionist measure. Suppose that a certain country excludes products produced in a foreign country to protect its critical infrastructures. This act may infringe "nondiscrimination principles" for free trade. The strengthening of supply chain resilience may also contravene the provision of state aid that bans governments from providing subsidies to reinforce their industry with low competitiveness. It may well happen that a certain country's supply chains are fragile. But there are reasons why they are so. If it is more efficient to produce necessary products in other countries than at home, it makes economic sense to import those products rather than to procure home products. State aid is allowed in cases of so-called "positive externalities," i.e., the realization of social values that could materialize if left to the market, such as the research and development of new technologies and environmental protection. In

---

[8] Khan (2020).
[9] Drezner et al. (2021).
[10] Harding (2017).
[11] Blackwill and Harris (2016).

some cases, security is also recognized as a "positive externality." These are "security exceptions," which, under the World Trade Organization (WTO) regime, are specified in General Agreement on Tariffs and Trade (GATT) Article 21, but such exceptions are applicable only in limited cases.

It is true that "security exceptions" stipulated by the Regional Comprehensive Economic Partnership (RCEP) and the Comprehensive and Progressive Agreement for Trans-Pacific Partnership (CPTPP) are subject to a broad range of interpretations; there is room for a state to arbitrarily decide what corresponds to security. On the other hand, the WTO security exception rules are extremely limiting; any infringement of their provisions is highly likely to be judged to not be in conformity with those rules by the WTO dispute settlement mechanism.

Meanwhile, the WTO is not fully functioning, partly because its Appellate Body members are not appointed due to U.S. opposition. Therefore, even if, for example, a member country's economic and security measures violate the WTO rules, no WTO mechanism is functional to identify and punish it. As a result, some countries including the United States consider that there is more legitimacy in strengthening their economic security and developing industrial policies in a way that protects their industry than in respecting the free trade regime and acting according to its rules. Likewise, as far as critical infrastructures are concerned, some member countries have come to consider it rational to exclude products manufactured in a particular country to prioritize their economic and social stability, rather than to emphasize the WTO's non-discrimination principles—even if such an exclusionist measure is discriminatory.

GATT Article 21 was written shortly after World War II and has rarely been questioned in association with the postwar order. During the Cold War, the free trade system developed mainly in the West due to the extreme scarcity of economic exchanges between the East and West. With the end of the Cold War, China's reform and opening-up efforts integrated the country into the international economy. In addition, its accession to the WTO in 2001 changed the situation dramatically. During the post-WWII and Cold War eras, there was no conflict between security issues and free trade issues because free trade was promoted by Western nations that shared identical security interests and values. When China joined the WTO, expectations were high that China would share the same interests and values as the Western nations and respect the interests and values of the liberal regime. In reality, however, China enjoyed economic benefits from the free trade system but rejected its values and remained within the free trade system, adhering to different values and ideologies. In addition, China's economic growth has helped raise its military power, which has emerged as a security concern. With these developments in the background, security issues came to the fore for the first time in the free trade block. (In the past, Russia and Ukraine[12] in one case and Saudi Arabia and Qatar[13] in another case filed a suit with the WTO over the application of security exceptions. But the WTO has so far not awarded a definitive ruling in either case.)

Conclusion

The term "economic security" is employed in various ways in Japan; the United States and Japan are at variance over how to define it. Different meanings given by so many parties could confuse the concept and lead to losing sight of the destination of the policy. To remove conceptual confusion and to promote helpful discussions, we should precisely exhibit our views on economic security when discussing it.

Economic security entails a wide gamut of meanings depending on the context it is used in. Yet, no matter how it is used, the contradiction that the concept harbors with the free trade system is apparent. Japan, which has rebuilt the Trans-Pacific Partnership (TPP) after the U.S. withdrawal and established the RCEP inclusive of China and South Korea, is now the leader of the free trade system and is in a position to lead the "rules-based international order." The proposed economic security bill pays great attention to the balance between economic security and free trade. It limits the implementation of the law to a much narrower area of industry: supply chain resilience should be limited to "strategically critical goods" and the protection of critical infrastructure should be limited to the "command and control systems." The rest of goods and services are to remain the subject of free trade. However, the definition of "strategically critical goods" is still arbitrary and opaque. Whether the contradiction between economic security and free trade can be solved or not remains to be seen in the implementation of the law.

References

Blackwill, R. D., & Harris, J. M. (2016). *War by other means: Geoeconomics and statecraft.* Belknap Press.
Blanchard, J.-M. F., & Ripsman, N. M. (2008, October). A political theory of economic statecraft. *Foreign Policy Analysis, 4*(4), 371–398.
Drezner, D. W., Farrell, H., & Newman, A. L. (Eds.). (2021). *The uses and abuses of weaponized interdependence.* Brookings Institution Press.
European Parliament. (2021, November). *Briefing: Resilience of global supply chains challenges and solutions,* PE 698.815. https://www.europarl.europa.eu/RegData/etudes/BRIE/2021/698 815/EPRS_BRI(2021)698815_EN.pdf

---

[12] Russia—Measures Concerning Traffic in Transit, Panel Report, WT/DS512/R (April 5, 2019). https://docs.wto.org/dol2fe/Pages/SS/directdoc.aspx?filename=q:/WT/DS/512R.pdf&Open=True.

[13] Saudi Arabia—Measures Concerning the Protection of Intellectual Property Rights, Report of the Panel, WT/DS567/R (16 June 2020). https://docs.wto.org/dol2fe/Pages/SS/directdoc.aspx?filename=q:/WT/DS/567R.pdf&Open=True.

Harding, R. (2017). *Weaponization of trade: The great unbalancing of politics and economics.* London Publishing Partnership.

Khan, S. M. (2020, October). *U.S. semiconductor exports to China: Current policies and trends, center for security and emerging technology.* https://cset.georgetown.edu/wp-content/uploads/U.S.-Semiconductor-Exports-to-China-Current-Policies-and-Trends.pdf

Liberal Democratic Party. (2020, December 16). *For setting up economic security strategy (Keizai-Anzen-Hosyo-Senryaku Seitei ni Mukete).* Policy Council. https://jimin.jp-east-2.storage.api.nifcloud.com/pdf/news/policy/201021_1.pdf

Liberal Democratic Party. (2021, May 27). *Proposal for "Basic direction for economic and financial management and their reform in FY 2021" (Keizai-Zaisei-Unei to Kaikaku no Kihon-Hoshin 2021).* Policy Council. https://jimin.jp-east-2.storage.api.nifcloud.com/pdf/news/policy/201648_1.pdf

Suzuki, K. (2021, December 3). What Japan needs to do to boost its economic security. *Japan Times.* https://www.japantimes.co.jp/opinion/2021/12/03/commentary/japan-commentary/japan-economic-security/

White House, Executive Order on America's Supply Chains, EO 14017. (2021, 24 February). https://www.whitehouse.gov/briefing-room/presidential-actions/2021/02/24/executive-order-on-americas-supply-chains/

Wilson, J. (2021, November 9). Australia shows the world what decoupling from China looks like. *Foreign Policy.* https://foreignpolicy.com/2021/11/09/australia-china-decoupling-trade-sanctions-coronavirus-geopolitics/

Open Access This chapter is licensed under the terms of the Creative Commons Attribution-NonCommercial-NoDerivatives 4.0 International License (http://creativecommons.org/licenses/by-nc-nd/4.0/), which permits any noncommercial use, sharing, distribution and reproduction in any medium or format, as long as you give appropriate credit to the original author(s) and the source, provide a link to the Creative Commons license and indicate if you modified the licensed material. You do not have permission under this license to share adapted material derived from this chapter or parts of it.

The images or other third party material in this chapter are included in the chapter's Creative Commons license, unless indicated otherwise in a credit line to the material. If material is not included in the chapter's Creative Commons license and your intended use is not permitted by statutory regulation or exceeds the permitted use, you will need to obtain permission directly from the copyright holder.

Chapter 12
The Future of the Liberal International Order

Hans Kundnani

Abstract Asia, Europe and the United States differ in their views about whether they should "decouple" from authoritarian states like China and Russia and thus defend a core liberal international order, or maintain an order that is "thinner" but universal. With these differences in their views on how to defend the liberal international order and how to respond to the rise of China, the U.S. is encouraged to build coalitions with a more inclusive approach to order-building rather than forcing allies to choose between itself and China. Germany and France aim to prioritize the rule-based order but are reluctant to emphasize democracy as the Biden administration does. Germany puts economic interests first, while France pursues an active military presence in the Pacific and aims to offer an alternative to a choice between China and the U.S. Those countries belonging to the Association of Southeast Asian Nations (ASEAN) are closer to the German position, while Australia, Japan, and India are becoming closer to the U.S. by prioritizing the trilateral security pact between Australia, the United Kingdom and the United States (AUKUS) and the Quadrilateral Security Dialogue (Quad).

In the last decade, there has been much discussion about the need to build a coalition of countries either to respond to the rise of China, or to defend the liberal international order, or both. But the essays in this collection illustrate some of the intellectual and political difficulties in doing so. They show that, as well as seeing the China challenge in different ways based on their own different interests and relationships with China, there are different views in Asia, Europe and the United States about the liberal international order itself. In particular, this concluding chapter examines differences around the sense in which the order is "liberal," different visions for the Indo-Pacific, and different views about whether the order should simply be defended or also reformed.

H. Kundnani (✉)
Europe Programme, Royal Institute of International Affairs, Chatham HouseLondon, UK

A Contested Concept

The liberal international order is an elusive concept that has been aptly referred to as "conceptual Jello-O."[1] That elusiveness has to do with the complexity of the order—it has different elements and it has evolved over time, particularly after the end of the Cold War.[2] But it is also has to do with an ambiguity about the sense in which the order that was created after World War II and developed in the post-Cold War period is "liberal." It can be understood as "liberal" in a political sense (that is, as opposed to authoritarianism), in an economic sense (that is, as opposed to economic nationalism or protectionism), or in an international relations sense (that is, as opposed to realism or other theories).

The idea of a liberal international order that is liberal in a political sense, which tends to be most prevalent in the United States, centers on democracy. If one thinks about the order in this way—in other words, that there is something inherently pro-democratic about it—the group of countries that have an interest in preserving it is largely synonymous with a coalition of democracies that some also argue is now needed and would be opposed to China and Russia as a kind of authoritarian axis. Thus, the questions of how to defend the order and how to respond to the China challenge merge; the idea is to build a coalition of countries that will do both.

The idea of a liberal international order that is liberal in the international relations sense, which tends to be most prevalent in Europe, centers on rules.[3] As Celine Pajon and Alexandra Sakaki point out, French and German policymakers both think in terms of the "rules-based order"—a term they prefer because they fear that the concept of "liberal international order" might alienate or antagonize non-democratic countries. The European emphasis on the importance of rules reflects a deeper desire to "domesticate" international politics embodied by the European Union itself, a regional rules-based order in which rules have gone further in replacing politics than elsewhere in the world in the last 40 years, albeit with some problematic consequences for democracy.[4]

Interestingly, as Richard McGregor points out, China also seems to prefer to talk about the "rules-based order," even if the prefix "so-called" expresses skepticism about the concept. China has a more complicated relationship with the existing system of rules than is often suggested. On the one hand, it is committed to the rules of the first iteration of the liberal international order after World War II in which state sovereignty was paramount. It has also benefited more than anyone from the "hyper-globalization" produced by the post-Cold War liberalization of the economic order. On the other hand, this new post-Cold war version of the order also undermined

---

[1] Allison (2018).

[2] See Kundnani (2017).

[3] Theorists of the liberal international order often see democracy and rule adherence as going together. For example, Ikenberry writes that "democracies are—in contrast to autocratic and authoritarian states—particularly able and willing to operate within an open, rule-based international system and to cooperate for mutual gain." Ikenberry (2011).

[4] See Kundnani (2018).

state sovereignty through principles like the Responsibility to Protect, which China opposes.

The complexity of the liberal international order helps to explain China's evolving approach to it. As China acquires and consolidates territory in the South China Seas and ignores international tribunal rulings, it is now threatening to break the rules on state sovereignty that it once criticized the United States for violating, as Russia already has. At the same time, as McGregor shows, it also wants to change the rules to better reflect its own interests—a legitimate aspiration from a realist perspective but less so from a liberal perspective. This creates a dilemma for others: should they seek to work with China to reform the liberal international order, or should they seek simply to defend it from China and perhaps even exclude China from it?

The dilemma is particularly relevant to the question of the liberalism of the liberal international order in an economic sense. In the post-Cold War period, the order became more liberal in this economic sense—in particular through the creation of the World Trade Organization, which was created in 1994, and which China joined in 2001. Initially, theorists of the liberal international order were hopeful that the integration of China into a system of free trade would transform China into a "responsible stakeholder" and strengthen the order.[5] But more recently, there has been a rethink as economic interdependence with China has come to be seen as a vulnerability as well as an opportunity.

Here, Japan is a particularly interesting case. It has created a new position of minister for economic security and, as Kazuto Suzuki shows, is taking steps to protect its key industries and infrastructure from embargoes and sanctions by other countries, especially China. But, as he rightly acknowledges, these steps should be understood as essentially protectionist. In that sense, they embody a partial rejection or reversal of the economic liberalism of the post-Cold War liberal international order. Of course, whether such steps are the beginning of a dangerous protectionist spiral or an overdue correction to the excessive economic liberalism of the post-Cold War order is a matter of debate.

Indo-Pacific Objectives

During the Trump administration, the United States saw the China challenge in largely realist terms. As Zack Cooper shows, the National Defense Strategy published in 2018 centered on the idea of "great power competition." But the Biden administration has reframed the challenge as part of a wider ideological struggle between democracy and authoritarianism. This ideological reframing may in theory create more space for allies in Asia and Europe to identify with the U.S. strategy. But many in both Asia and Europe are skeptical of the democracy framing, which they see as too adversarial and binary. As we have seen, it is also for these reasons that France and Germany prefer the idea of a "rules-based" order to a "liberal" one.

---

[5] See for example Ikenberry (2008).

There are striking differences even between French and German approaches to the Indo-Pacific. Sakaki writes that above all Germany seeks to "preserve peace and stability" in the Indo-Pacific—not least so it can continue to export there—but until recently did little to contribute to security in the region. France's approach is almost the opposite. Pajon writes that, as a nuclear power and permanent member of the United Nations Security Council that also has extensive territory and 1.5 million citizens in the Indo-Pacific, its focus is primarily on "the security dimension of the rules-based order." Along with the United Kingdom, but unlike most other EU member states, it has been willing to carry out presence operations in the Indo-Pacific.

However, the German view of the Indo-Pacific is strikingly similar to that of south-eastern Asian countries—and indeed German policymakers see the Association of Southeast Asian Nations (ASEAN) as an important and promising partner in the region. Nithin Coca argues that south-east Asian countries are predominantly focused on their economic interests and are "unable or unwilling to take an active role" in protecting the liberal international order. However, as he shows, they do need alternatives to Chinese investment and the Chinese market. This is where Europeans and especially Germans think they can help—in particular through the EU connectivity strategy that Maaike Okano-Heijmans discusses in her chapter.

For France, however, the partnership between ASEAN and the EU forms part of a wider idea that the EU could be a *puissance d'équilibre*, or balancing power, that would offer an alternative to the choice between China and the United States that countries around the world but especially in the Indo-Pacific increasingly seem to face. "Rather than upholding a continued U.S. dominance," Pajon writes, "France supports a multipolar order that would allow for it to pursue its own approach, while also reducing China's influence in the region." In other words, it is not just that continental Europeans "perceive an increasingly multipolar world," as Cooper puts it, but that some, particularly in France, want actively to create an order that is more multipolar.

France had originally hoped that India and even Australia and Japan might be part of such an alternative grouping pursuing a "third path" in the Indo-Pacific. But the the trilateral security pact between Australia, the United Kingdom and the United States (AUKUS) announced in 2021 shattered illusions that Australia might join France in seeking an alternative to a U.S.-led approach. As a U.S. treaty ally, Japan is also unlikely to be a candidate for an alternative grouping. India has traditionally sought to be "non-aligned," which makes it a more promising partner for France. But as Dhruva Jaishankar shows, while India is interested in deepening partnerships with countries like France, it sees them as complementing the Quadrilateral Security Dialogue (Quad) rather than as an alternative to it. France will likely face a choice between deepening cooperation with Quad countries or remaining without close partners in the region, except perhaps ASEAN.

As Luis Simon shows, the Euro-Atlantic and Indo-Pacific are increasingly interconnected, which could create a basis for Europeans to make more of a contribution to security in the Indo-Pacific. But the French aspiration to be a balancing power— that is, not so much to uphold the U.S.-led order that Simon describes as to create an alternative to it—will remain a major barrier to the development of a joint Transatlantic approach to the China challenge and/or the Indo-Pacific. Pajon suggests that French or EU policy could actually "complement" a U.S. approach that is more focused on using military power to deter China from aggressive actions. But as her chapter makes clear, the idea of a balancing power is based not on the use of different tools for the same objectives but rather on different objectives.

Beyond a Defensive Approach

Perhaps because China seeks to reform the liberal international order, there is a reflexive tendency in the West to simply defend it as it is. This is most clearly expressed by Europeans—Sakaki says that Germany seeks to "defend" the order and Pajon says that France seeks to "preserve" it. However, the United Kingdom's Integrated Review, published in 2021, suggests it is moving away from the idea of defending a "rules-based order" and towards a different approach. In a more competitive world, the review said, "a defence of the status quo is no longer sufficient."[6] Instead, together with its partners but taking a lead where it can, the U.K. needed to take a much more proactive and dynamic approach to shape the world.

Even if increased competition did not require it, however, there are good reasons to think we need to go beyond a defensive approach to the liberal international order. In particular, it is now clear that the way the order evolved in the post-Cold War period had problematic consequences both domestically and internationally that in turn helped undermine support for the order in the United States, the main guarantor of the order. In other words, instead of simply defending the liberal international order, we need to reform it. In particular, there is a need to reform the economic order, which became even more liberal during the post-Cold War period.

Cooper argues that the liberal international order needs to be adapted for an era of multipolarity. He writes that the United States should accept the reality that the world is multipolar and seek to "build coalitions rather than attract countries into the U.S. orbit." In other words, countries would not be forced to choose between China and the United States. This would go some way to meeting French, German and south-east Asian concerns about the increasing "polarization" of international politics. But although this might be a "more inclusive approach to order-building," as Cooper suggests, it leaves open the question of what a reformed liberal international order itself would look like.

The dilemma that the United States and its allies ultimately face, and which runs through the essays in this collection, is whether to continue to seek to include China and other authoritarian states in the liberal international order. John Ikenberry has

---

[6] Global Britain in a Competitive Age. The Integrated Review of Security, Defence, Development and Foreign Policy (March 2021) p. 11, https://www.gov.uk/government/publications/global-britain-in-a-competitive-age-the-integrated-review-of-security-defence-development-and-foreign-policy.

shown how the liberal international order began as an "inside order" within the U.S. alliance system and then expanded in the post-Cold War period to include other states.[7] The accession of China to the World Trade Organization was the defining moment of this expansion of the liberal international order. Now that the problematic consequences of that expansion have become clearer, the choice is whether to "decouple" from those states, and thus shrink the order back to something like its original core, or to maintain an order that is "thinner" but universal.[8]

References

Allison, G. (2018). *The myth of the liberal order*. Foreign Affairs. https://www.foreignaffairs.com/united-states/myth-liberal-order

Ikenberry, G. J. (2011). *Liberal leviathan: The origins, crisis, and transformation of the American world order* (p. 63). Princeton University Press.

Ikenberry. (2008). *The rise of China and the future of the west*. Foreign Affairs.

Kundnani, H. (2017). *What is the liberal international order?* German Marshall Fund. https://www.gmfus.org/news/what-liberal-international-order

Kundnani, H. (2018). *When the rules won't bend*. The World Today. https://www.chathamhouse.org/when-rules-wont-bend

Niblett, R. (2017). *Liberalism in retreat*. Foreign Affairs (2017).

Open Access This chapter is licensed under the terms of the Creative Commons Attribution-NonCommercial-NoDerivatives 4.0 International License (http://creativecommons.org/licenses/by-nc-nd/4.0/), which permits any noncommercial use, sharing, distribution and reproduction in any medium or format, as long as you give appropriate credit to the original author(s) and the source, provide a link to the Creative Commons license and indicate if you modified the licensed material. You do not have permission under this license to share adapted material derived from this chapter or parts of it.

The images or other third party material in this chapter are included in the chapter's Creative Commons license, unless indicated otherwise in a credit line to the material. If material is not included in the chapter's Creative Commons license and your intended use is not permitted by statutory regulation or exceeds the permitted use, you will need to obtain permission directly from the copyright holder.

---

[7] See Ikenberry, *Liberal Leviathan*. Op. Cit.

[8] On a "thinner" order, see Niblett (2017).

The manufacturer's authorised representative in the EU is Springer Nature Customer Service Centre GmbH, Europaplatz 3, 69115 Heidelberg, Germany. If you have any concerns regarding our products, please contact ProductSafety@springernature.com

Printed and bound by CPI Group (UK) Ltd, Croydon, CR0 4YY

25/03/2026

02078170-0014